DUMB
DAD
JOKES

DUMB
DAD
JOKES

Something for Everyone
from Ages 6 to 106

Reader's
Digest

New York / Montreal

A READER'S DIGEST BOOK

Copyright ©2019 Trusted Media Brands, Inc.
All rights reserved. Unauthorized reproduction, in any manner, is prohibited.
Reader's Digest is a registered trademark of Trusted Media Brands, Inc.

Library of Congress Cataloging-in-Publication Data is available on request.

ISBN 978-1-62145-430-4

Cover design: George McKeon
Cover and all spot illustrations: Vainui de Castelbajac
Cartoon Credits: Ian Baker: *154;* John Caldwell: *32, 62, 77;* Dave Carpenter:
17, 25, 90, 98, 204; Vainui de Castelbajac: *6, 9, 28, 31, 53, 75, 89, 113, 133, 153,
169, 173, 195 and all spot art;* Ken Catalino: *159, 196;* Joe di Chiarro: *174, 189;*
Roy Delgado: *37, 48, 115;* Ralph Hagen: *20, 135, 138;* Mike Lynch: *45, 128, 162
181;* Scott Arthur Masear: *108;* Harley Schwadron: *212;* Steve Smeltzer: *85,
105, 201;* Thomas Bros.: *40, 55, 59, 67, 72, 80, 123, 143, 148, 184;*
Kim Warp: *12;* Elizabeth Westley & Steven Mach: *95, 118, 209*

We are committed to both the quality of our products and the
service we provide to our customers. We value your comments,
so please feel free to contact us.

Reader's Digest Adult Trade Publishing
44 S. Broadway
White Plains, NY 10601

For more Reader's Digest products and information, visit our website:
www.rd.com (in the United States)
www.readersdigest.ca (in Canada)

Printed in China

1 3 5 7 9 10 8 6 4 2

contents

A NOTE FROM THE **EDITORS**

"Happiness is having a large, loving, caring,
close-knit family in another city."

GEORGE BURNS

Ah, family. They are there for us in good times and
bad, ready to lend a hand or offer a shoulder to cry
on. They see us at our best and our worst, and, if we are
lucky, they accept us just as we are. If we are equally lucky,
they help us find the humor in life as well—or unknowingly
provide it.

Here at Reader's Digest, we have always turned to
humor to bring us together, and over the years we've
found that our readers do the same thing. Whether they
are sharing the challenges of raising children or aging
gracefully; surviving the holidays or a family vacation; or
struggling with new-fangled math or the politics of a little
league game, readers enjoy laughing at family foibles—
their own and others'.

In *Reader's Digest Dumb Dad Jokes* we have curated
some of the funniest family stories, jokes, anecdotes,
and riddles in order to remind readers that no matter the
situation, one can always rely on family to offer some
comic relief. We hope you'll grab your family—everyone
from ages 6 to 106—and share the gags and funny
moments in this book and be reassured that home is
where the heart is—and the humor.

ALL IN THE
FAMILY

❝ Always be nice to your children because they are the ones who will choose your rest home. ❞

PHYLLIS DILLER

EVERYBODY **LOVES MOM**

My cousin was in love and wanted to introduce his bride-to-be to his hypercritical mother. But in order to get an unbiased opinion, he invited over three other female friends as well and didn't tell his mom which one he intended to marry.

After the four women left, he asked his mother, "Can you guess which one I want to marry?"

"The one with short hair."

"Yes! How'd you know?"

"Because that's the one I didn't like."

● FATIMA FARHAT

Eight months into my pregnancy, I was being bombarded with kicks from inside the womb.

"He sure keeps his feet busy," I said to my husband one day. "Maybe he'll be a soccer player. Or a dancer. What do you think he'll be?"

"Hard to keep up with," my husband quipped.

● ELENA BAKER

On our way to my parents' house for dinner one evening, I glanced over at my fifteen-year-old daughter. "Isn't that skirt a bit short?" I asked.

She rolled her eyes at my comment and gave me one of those "Oh, Mom" looks.

When we arrived at my folks' place, my mother greeted us at the door, hugged my daughter, then turned to me and said, "Elizabeth! Don't you think that blouse is awfully low-cut?"

● ELIZABETH SCOTT

One evening I was commenting on my bad exercise habits and tight clothes. Whenever I criticize myself, my four-year-old son always has something charming to say.

Using a new word this time, he smiled and said, "Oh, no, Mommy! You look flabulous!"

● JILLYNNE M. BAILEY

> My mother had a great deal of trouble with me, but I think she enjoyed it.
>
> MARK TWAIN

I'm forever asking my family to repeat what they say. Convinced that I had a hearing problem, I grudgingly went to a specialist to be tested.

After running all the tests, the doctor said, "Your hearing is exceptional. Your problem is that you live with a husband and three teenagers who all mumble."

● LINDA GAUTHIER

A couple invited some people to dinner. At the table, the wife turned to their six-year-old daughter and said, "Would you like to say the blessing?"

"I wouldn't know what to say," the girl replied.

"Just say what you hear Mommy say," the wife answered.

The daughter bowed her head and said, "Lord, why on earth did I invite all these people to dinner?"

I was on my way out of the house to meet with a cantankerous client, and I was dreading it. The look on my face must have given me away because my four-year-old daughter asked what was wrong.

"I'm going to meet a woman who always yells at Daddy," I told her.

"Oh," she said. "Say hi to Mom."

● BART KEY

Why Babies Can't Talk

For the first time, my four-year-old daughter Kelsey was coming to my office to have me, a dental hygienist, clean her teeth. She was accompanied by her grandmother. When they came in, I greeted them warmly, seated Kelsey and, as usual, put on my gloves, goggles and mask. About ten minutes into the procedure, she got scared and cried, "I want my mommy!"

I quickly pulled off my mask and said, "I am your mommy."

Without hesitating, my daughter yelled back, "Then I want my granny!"

● LAURIE GOFF

My mother is always trying to understand what motivates people, especially those in her family. One day she and my sister were talking about one relative's bad luck. "Why do you suppose she changed jobs?" Mother asked my sister. "Maybe she has a subconscious desire not to succeed."

"Or maybe it just happened," said my sister, exasperated. "Do you know you analyze everything to death?"

Mother was silent for a moment. "That's true," she said. "Why do you think I do that?"

● BOBBIE S. CYPHERS

I was on the couch nursing my newborn when my three-year-old plopped down to watch. Seeing this as a good teaching moment, I explained how mothers feed their babies. My daughter's eyes grew wider with each detail.

"She's drinking milk?" she asked. "In the living room?!"

● BEVERLY FRIEND

One rainy morning, my mother went for her daily run. As she returned to the house, she slipped and fell, hitting her head on the driveway.

I called the paramedics. When they arrived, they asked my mom some questions to determine her coherency.

"What is today?" inquired one man.

Without hesitation, Mom replied, "Trash day."

● JAIME SWART

A Freudian slip is when you say one thing but mean your mother.

I can't tell the difference between a rose and a dandelion. So when it came time to fix up my garden, I had no clue which plants to keep and which ones to remove. Until, that is, my mother gave me this handy tip: "Pull them all up. If it comes back, it's a weed."

● CY COGGINS

During a science lesson, my sister-in-law picked up a magnet and said to her second-grade class, "My name begins with the letter M, and I pick things up. What am I?"

A little boy answered, "You're a mommy."

● ROBERT BOYER

While driving on the highway, my daughter noticed a child in the window of a car in the next lane, holding up a handwritten sign that read "Help."

A few minutes later, the car passed her and she again glanced at it. The little boy held up the same sign and this time followed it with another, which read, "My mother is singing!"

● LIL GIBSON

I was a stay-at-home mom when my kids were young. One day, I had a mid-afternoon appointment, and so I asked the kids to leave a note if they went out after school.

My eleven-year-old daughter, Karen, left me this note:

> Dear Mom,
> Claudette is at the youth group.
> Ernie is playing road hockey.
> Donna's at Wendy's and I'm at the bars.
> Love, Karen.

She had returned to school to play on the monkey bars!

● FLO GAUDET

FATHER KNOWS BEST?

When a squirrel slipped into my house, I did the logical thing: I panicked and called my father.

"How do you get a squirrel out of a basement?" I shrieked.

Dad advised me to leave a trail of peanut butter and crackers from the basement to the outside. It worked—the squirrel ate his way out of the house. Unfortunately, he passed another squirrel eating his way in.

● CORINNE STEVENS

Max the little camel walks into his parents' room at 3 a.m. and asks for a glass of water.

"Another one?" says his father. "That's the second glass this month."

It began as an innocent game with my toddler son, Robert. I'd get in the fighter's stance and start shadowboxing. Jabbing with both fists, I'd say, "One-two, one-two," and he would imitate me over and over.

I never thought about the consequences of this little exercise until my wife took our son to a birthday party. When the boy's mother was handing out noisemakers she leaned over to Robert and asked, "Would you like one too?"

It took my wife a while to explain her way out of what happened next.

● ALFRED ISNARDI

My father is allergic to cotton. He has pills that he can take, but he can't get them out of the bottle.

Our priest asked how things were going with my father. "Well, he has issues," I replied, then shared a few details.

After listening, he said, "Issues? Sounds like he's got a year's subscription."

● LAURIE LALDO

No one is more cautious than a first-time parent. After our daughter was big enough to ride on the back of my bicycle, I bought a special carrier with a seat belt and got her a little helmet. The day of the first ride I put her in the seat, double-checked all the equipment, wheeled the bike to the end of the driveway, carefully looked both ways and, swinging my leg up over the crossbar, accidentally kicked her in the chin.

● ZACHARY GIBBS

A friend of mine has an adopted son who, at six-foot-one, loves to play basketball. The boy was applying to basketball camp, and a section of the application called for him to write a brief essay about himself. My friend got a lump in his throat as he read his son's words: "Most of all I am thankful that I am adopted . . ."

Then my friend got a cold dose of reality as he continued: "because my dad is so short."

● RALPH G. LOCKERBIE

THE DAY I KNEW MY IN-LAWS HAD FINALLY ACCEPTED ME:

As we pulled into their driveway, my father-in-law was on the phone. "Oh, I have to run," he told the person on the other end. "My daughter-in-law and her husband just arrived."

● KATHY DIERKER

"Thanks for the talk, Dad. But I was asking about the birds and bees for my zoology test."

My husband was bending over to tie my three-year-old's shoes. That's when I noticed my son, Ben, staring at my husband's head.

He gently touched the slightly thinning spot of hair and said in a concerned voice, "Daddy, you have a hole in your head. Does it hurt?"

After a pause, I heard my husband's murmured reply: "Not physically."

● LAURIE GERHARDSTEIN

Dad is from the old school, where you keep your money under the mattress—only he kept his in the underwear drawer. One day I bought my dad an unusual personal safe—a can of spray paint with a false bottom—so he could keep his money in the workshop. Later I asked Mom if he was using it.

"Oh, yes," she replied, "he put his money in it the same day."

"No burglar would think to look on the work shelf!" I gloated.

"They won't have to," my mom replied. "He keeps the paint can in his underwear drawer."

● JUDEE MULVEY

I'd like to have a kid, but I'm not sure I'm ready to spend ten years of my life constantly asking someone where his shoes are.

● @DAMIENFAHEY

There should be a children's song: "If you're happy and you know it, keep it to yourself and let your dad sleep."

● JIM GAFFIGAN, COMEDIAN

My five children and I were playing hide-and-seek one evening. With the lights turned off in the house, the kids scattered to hide, and I was "it." After a few minutes I located all of them. When it was my turn to hide, they searched high and low but could not find me.

Finally one of my sons got a bright idea. He went to the phone and dialed; they found me immediately because my phone started ringing.

● **LELEND JENSEN**

> I want to have a kid the way other people want to own stock in Google: I don't want to be responsible for it; I just want to go to parties and talk about how well it's doing.
>
> COMIC RAQUEL D'APICE

An elderly gentleman with a hearing problem goes to an audiologist, who fits him with hearing aids. A month later, the man returns to the doctor for a checkup. "Your hearing is almost perfect," the doctor remarks. "Your family must be really pleased you can hear again."

"Oh, I haven't told them yet," the gentleman replies, "I just sit around and listen to their conversations. I've changed my will three times so far!"

● **ROY THIRWELL WARNER**

Our family took shelter in the basement after hearing a tornado warning. My husband told everyone to stay put while he got his cell phone out of the car, in case the lines went dead.

He didn't return for the longest time, so I went looking for him. I was upstairs calling his name, when I heard our phone machine click on.

"Hi," a voice said. "This is Dad. I'm locked out of the house."

● **LAURE JORGES**

When my father ran out of gas, he called my mother to pick him up in her car. They went to a gas station, filled a gas can, and returned to his car. After a few minutes, he got into her car again. "We need to go back to the gas station," he said.

"One gallon wasn't enough?" she asked.

"It would have been if I'd put it in the right car."

● KENT T. CRITCHLOW

When I bought my new Lexus Sport Coupe, my two sons asked me who would inherit it if I met my demise. I pondered the question, then told them if I passed away on an even day, the son born on an even day would get it. If it happened on an odd day, the one born on the odd day would get it.

A few weekends later, while river rafting with one of my sons, I was tossed out of the boat. As I floated in the rapids, I heard my son yelling, "It's the wrong day!"

● GREG ZARET

One night about 10 p.m., I answered the phone and heard, "Dad, we want to stay out late. Is that okay?"

"Sure," I answered, "as long as you called."

When I hung up, my wife asked who was on the phone.

"One of the boys," I replied. "I gave them permission to stay out late."

"Not our boys," she said. "They're both downstairs in the basement."

● LAWRENCE M. WEISBERG

I have mixed emotions when I receive Father's Day gifts. I'm glad my children remember me, but I'm disappointed that they actually think I dress that way.

● COMIC MIKE DUGAN

BLOOD IS THICKER THAN WATER

My mom had always wanted to learn to play the piano, so Dad bought her one for her birthday. A few weeks later, I called and asked how she was doing. "We returned the piano," said Dad. "I persuaded her to switch to a clarinet."

"Why?" I asked.

"Because," he explained, "with a clarinet, she can't sing along."

● DON FOSTER

Before my daughter went on her first date, I gave her "the talk."

"Sometimes, it's easy to get carried away when you're with a boy," I said. "Remember, a short moment of indiscretion could ruin your life."

"Don't worry," she said. "I don't plan on ruining my life until I get married."

● CYNDI LASALA

My grandmother, Odette, is an avid knitter and a true Canadian. She knits throughout the winter, sitting in front of the TV. Despite having given her tokens of love away for free to family and friends, her knitting outpaced her giving and she decided to start selling her wares. Grandma asked me how much she should charge for each item. I asked her how long it took her to knit something and she replied, "Well, scarves take me about a hockey game and a half, and the hats take me just over two games."

● NATHALIE GOUGEON

My husband and I both work, so our family eats out a lot. Recently, when we were having a rare home-cooked meal, I handed a glass to my three-year-old and told her to drink her milk.

She looked at me bewildered and replied, "But I didn't order milk."

● JANET A. NUSSBAUM

To keep their active two-year-old from roaming onto the busy street in front of their home, my sister and brother-in-law decided to put a gate across the driveway. After working over two weekends on the project, Robert was ready to attach the lock to complete the job. He was working on the yard side of the gate, with his daughter nearby, when he dropped the screwdriver he was using and it rolled under the gate, out of his reach.

"I'll get it, Daddy," Lauren called, nimbly crawling under the newly erected barrier.

● JANICE DECOSTE

My sister is a know-it-all who bristles at anyone's well-intentioned advice. But when our older sister gave her several clever tips, she was impressed. "I have to hand it to Pat," she told me. "She really is smart. Not Jeopardy! smart; more Wheel of Fortune smart."

● TERESA BRUCE

"I need to talk to you" is the one sentence that has the power to make you remember every bad thing you've ever done in your life.

● AARON KARO, ON RUMINATIONS.COM

While I was dining out with my children, a man came over to our table and we started talking. He asked where my kids go to school. I told him we home-school them. With a raised eyebrow he asked if my husband is the sole breadwinner for our family. I said no, I also work—out of our home. Then, noticing our two-month-old son, he mentioned that his daughter had just had a baby, and he wondered what hospital our son was born in.

"He was born at home," I answered.

The man looked at me, then said, "Wow, you don't get out much, do you?"

● LAURA HANSER

One evening after dinner, my five-year-old son Brian noticed that his mother had gone out. In answer to his questions, I told him, "Mommy is at a Tupperware party."

This explanation satisfied him for only a moment. Puzzled, he asked, "What's a Tupperware party, Dad?"

I've always given my son honest answers, so I figured a simple explanation would be the best approach. "Well, Brian," I said, "at a Tupperware party, a bunch of ladies sit around and sell plastic bowls to each other."

Brian nodded, indicating that he understood. Then he burst into laughter. "Come on, Dad," he said. "What is it really?"

● KENNETH W. HOLMES

A family is a unit composed not only of children but of men, women, an occasional animal, and the common cold.

● OGDEN NASH

As the result of an explosive argument with our mother, my little brother pasted a sign reading "I hate Mom" on the door to his room, and slammed it shut.

My dad, a school psychologist, came home after work to this tense standoff. "I'll take care of it," he confidently told Mom, and went into my brother's room. Minutes later, Dad came out. "He doesn't hate you anymore," he reassured her.

Sure enough, my brother had crossed out "Mom" on his sign. It now read "I hate Dad."

● MICHELE PECORARO

Since I am a busy mom of four, I rely on my children to help me out with everyday chores around the house. One morning I was running around trying to get the children and myself ready, when I suddenly realized it was trash pickup day. So I handed a bag of garbage to my sleepy seven-year-old son and told him to toss it in the trash bin on his way out the door.

Glancing out my window moments later, I saw him wearily boarding the bus. He was carrying his backpack, his lunchbox and a big white bag of garbage.

● LYNN PAREJKO

As she slid behind the wheel for her first driving lesson, my daughter couldn't contain her excitement. "You need to make adjustments so the car is comfortable for you, the driver," I began. "Now, what's the first thing you should do?"

"Change the radio station," she said.

● RHONDA BUCALO

I was about to leave the house on an errand, and my husband was getting ready for a dental appointment. "I wish we could trade places," I said, knowing how much he dreaded the coming ordeal.

He watched as I gathered our newborn onto my left arm and picked up a package with that hand. I flung a diaper bag and my purse over my right shoulder, grabbed our two-year-old with my free hand and wrestled the car keys from him.

My husband shook his head. "No, thanks," he said. "At least where I'm going they give you anesthesia."

● LINDA CHIARA

"My great-grandma gave me this money," said my three-year-old, happily clutching a $20 bill he'd gotten as a present.

"That's right," I said. "How did you know that?"

Pointing to Andrew Jackson's face in the middle, he said, "Because her picture is on it."

● ANDI OLSON

Sean, my son, was twelve when he first decided to do his own laundry. He called me at work to ask how much soap to use. "About a capful," I replied.

I arrived home a few hours later to find suds halfway up the basement stairs. "How much soap did you use?" I said, gaping at the mess.

"Only a capful," he said sheepishly, holding a damp baseball cap.

● MARY LOU COGHLAN

As my fortieth birthday approached, my husband, who is a year younger, was doing his best to rub it in. Trying to figure out what all the teasing was about, our young daughter asked me, "How old is Daddy?"

"Thirty-nine," I told her.

"And how old will you be?"

"Forty," I said sadly.

"But Mommy," she exclaimed, "you're winning!"

● KELLEY MARTINEZ

A two-year-old is kind of like having a blender, but you don't have a top for it.

● JERRY SEINFELD

"Kevin, your mom and I have decided it's about time you moved out."

Our twenty-five-year-old son moved back home with an eye toward socking away money to buy a condo. We never bothered asking how long he'd planned to stay, but I got a pretty good idea when I walked into his room recently. In the corner was a milk jug with a few coins in it and a label that read "Condo down payment."

● TERESITA CORCUERA

It seemed that all our appliances had broken in the same week, and repairs were straining our budget. So when I picked up the kids from school and our Jeep started making rattling sounds, I decided that rather than burden my husband, I'd deal with it. I hadn't reckoned on my little tattletales, however. They rushed into the house with the news: "Daddy, the Jeep was breaking down, but Mom made the noise stop!"

Impressed, my husband asked, "How did you fix it?"

"I turned up the volume on the radio," I confessed.

● RUTH TEN VEEN

> My kids always perceived the bathroom as a place where you wait it out until all the groceries are unloaded from the car.
>
> ERMA BOMBECK

When a family friend passed away, my granddaughter took her three-year-old son to visit the widow. As they approached the front door, she whispered to the boy, "Make sure to tell her how sorry you are."

He whispered back, "Why, I didn't kill him."

● CHARLES GILDERSLEEVE

Our friend tells everyone that he began losing his hair while serving in Vietnam. His granddaughter incorporated that information into her grade school history report on the war. She wrote, "My Grandpa went to Vietnam and got his hair shot off."

● DARLENE KERANEN

Happiness is having a large, loving, caring, close-knit family in another city.

● GEORGE BURNS

My two-year-old cousin scared us one summer by disappearing during our lakeside vacation. More than a dozen relatives searched the forest and shoreline, and everyone was relieved when we found Matthew playing calmly in the woods.

"Listen to me, Matthew," his mother said sharply. "From now on when you want to go someplace, you tell Mommy first, okay?"

Matthew thought about that for a moment and said, "Okay. Disney World."

● LEAH HALLENBECK

Over dinner, I explained the health benefits of a colorful meal to my family. "The more colors, the more variety of nutrients," I told them. Pointing to our food, I asked, "How many different colors do you see?"

"Six," volunteered my daughter. "Seven if you count the burned parts."

● ALLISON BEVANS

RIDDLE
ME THIS!

" I think I am, therefore, I am. I think. **"**

GEORGE CARLIN

Q: Where does a king keep his armies?

A: In his sleevies!

● SAM ROBERTS

Q: What did the Zero say to the Eight?

A: "Nice belt!"

● TRACI OHREN

Q: What do you get from a pampered cow?

A: Spoiled milk.

● DUSTIN GODSEY

Q: What kind of coat is always wet when you put it on?

A: A coat of paint.

Q: What has 13 hearts, but no other organs?

A: A deck of playing cards.

Q: Why was the chef embarrassed?

A: Because he saw the salad dressing!

Q: What do you call an old snowman?

A: Water!

Q: What does Charles Dickens keep in his spice rack?

A: The best of thymes, the worst of thymes.

Q: What's the difference between a cat and a comma?

A: A cat has claws at the end of paws; a comma is a pause at the end of a clause.

Q: Which dinosaur knew the most words?

A: The thesaurus.

Q: Who did Frankenstein's monster bring to prom?

A: His ghoulfriend.

Q: Why do artists constantly feel cold?

A: Because they're surrounded by drafts.

Q: Did you hear the one about the convict who had an allergy?

A: He broke out.

● JAMES BRINK

Q: What does a nosey pepper do?

A: Gets jalapeño business!

Q: What lies at the bottom of the ocean and twitches?

A: A nervous wreck.

Q: What do you call a fish with no eye?

A: Fsh.

Q: Why can't a woman ask her brother for help?

A: Because he can't be a brother and assist her too.

Q: Why should you not mix alcohol and calculus?

A: Because you should never drink and derive.

Q: Why do bicycles fall over?

A: Because they are two-tired.

Q: How does Moses make tea?

A: He brews.

Q: Why did the children call St. Nick "Santa Caus"?

A: Because there was Noël.

Q: What is a lion's favorite Christmas carol?

A: Jungle Bells.

Q: Why are Comet, Cupid, Donner, and Blitzen always wet?

A: Because they are rain deer.

I have a fear of speed bumps, but I'm slowly getting over it.

● @RICKCOUCHMAN

Q: With pointed fangs I sit and wait; with piercing force I crunch out fate; grabbing victims, proclaiming might; physically joining with a single bite. What am I?

A: A stapler.

Just when I discovered the meaning of life, they changed it.

GEORGE CARLIN

Q: Why was Santa's little helper feeling depressed?

A: He had low elf-esteem.

Q: What did the bald man exclaim when he received a comb for a present?

A: "Gee, I'll never part with it!"

Q: Which trigonometric functions do farmers like?

A: Swine and cowswine.

Q: What did the Buddhist say to the pizza guy?

A: Make me one with everything.

Q: Did you hear about the giant who threw up?

A: It's all over town.

Q: What do you get when you cross the Atlantic Ocean with the Titanic?

A: Halfway.

Q: Why are cowboy hats turned up on the sides?

A: So that three people can fit in the pickup.

Q: Why were all the ink spots crying?

A: Their father was in the pen.

Q: Why can't you explain puns to kleptomaniacs?

A: They always take things literally.

Q: Why does Santa have three garden plots up at the North Pole?

A: That way he can hoe, hoe, hoe!

Q: What do fish say when they hit a concrete wall?

A: Dam!

● DUSTIN GODSEY

Q: What is an index?

A: It's what you wash windows with.

● JESSICA SHEEHAN

Q: Use the word baron in a sentence.

A: Mrs. Jones is baron and can't have children.

● MARCIA SHEALEY

Q: The War of 1812 was between . . .

A: 1811 and 1813.

● MELISSA SORGEN

Q: You're riding a horse at full speed. You're being chased by a lion and there's a giraffe in the way in front of you. How will you escape this highly dangerous situation?

A: Get off the carousel.

● STEPHANIE FINLAYSON

Q: How do you keep a bagel from getting away?

A: Put lox on it.

Q: What did one eye say to the other?

A: "Don't look now, but something between us smells."

Q: What do you call a Far Eastern monk who sells reincarnations?

A: A used karma dealer.

Q: Did you hear about the cell phones that got married?

A: The wedding was terrible, but the reception was terrific.

Q: Who delivers Christmas presents to good little sharks when they're sleeping?

A: Santa Jaws!

"Go sit in WHAT corner?"

Q: Why does a man twist his wedding ring on his finger?

A: He's trying to figure out the combination.

    ● ADAM JOSHUA SMARGON

Q: How was copper wire invented?

A: Two lawyers were fighting over a penny.

    ● TERRY SANGSTER

Q: Can you name three consecutive days without using the words Wednesday, Friday or Sunday?

A: Of course, you can—yesterday, today and tomorrow!

    ● CLAUDINE BAKKER

> I'm against picketing, but I don't know how to show it.
>
> MITCH HEDBERG

Q: Why was the math book sad?
A: Because it had so many problems.

Q: How do radios greet each other?
A: With airwaves.

Q: How can you tell a poker player is lying?
A: His chips are moving.

Q: How many folk musicians does it take to change a light bulb?
A: Four. One to change the bulb and the other three to sing about how good the old one was.

Q: Why did the elephant hate to play cards in the jungle?
A: Because there were too many cheetahs.

Q: What's the difference between a large cheese pizza and a poker player?
A: A large cheese pizza can feed a family of four.

Q: Did you hear about the two thieves who stole a calendar?
A: They got six months each.

Q: What did the ill comic say in the hospital?
A: "I'm here . . . all weak!

Q: What do you call memory loss in parrots?
A: Polynesia.

Q: Did you hear about the tree's birthday?
A: It was a sappy one.

Q: What did the slug say to the passing snail?
A: "Big Issue, mate?"

Q: What do you call a gorilla wearing earmuffs?
A: Anything you want. He can't hear you.

Q: Why does the ocean roar?

A: You would too if you had lobsters in your bed.

● DOUG BOWMAN

Q: What do you call a long row of floppy-eared mammals, all slowly hopping backwards together into the distance?

A: A receding hare-line.

● ELSPETH MCVIE

Q: What hides in the garden shed and trembles?

A: A nervous rake.

● MICHAEL SHILLITO

Q: What do you get when you cross a snake with a rabbit and an amoeba?

A: An adder that can multiply and divide.

● JOHN DRATWA

Q: What do you call a woman with a bottle opener in one hand, a knife in the other, a pair of scissors under her arm and a corkscrew behind her ear?

A: Swiss Army Wife.

● ANDREW BERRY

Q: What type of scientist digs through dirt until he finds treasure?

A: A psychologist.

● GAIL CHOATE

Q: What do most people do on a date?

A: On the first date they just tell each other lies and that usually gets them interested enough to go for a second date.

● MARTIN, AGE 10

If athletes get athlete's foot, do astronauts get mistletoe?

Q: What do you think your Mom and Dad have in common?

A: Both don't want any more kids.

● LORI, AGE 8

Q: Did you hear about the magic tractor?

A: It turned into a field.

● STEPHEN EDMISTON

Q: Give an example of a stereotype.

A: Sony.

● NICOLE HUGHES

"Why the heck do we have wings anyway?"

Q: What is a mammogram?

A: That's when people get their initials put on towels.

● PATRICIA RYAN-CURRY

Q: What do you call jewelry lost on the golf course?

A: A diamond in the rough.

● MARCIANO LEE

Q: How do you decide who to marry?

A: No person really decides before they grow up who they're going to marry. God decides it all way before, and you get to find out later who you're stuck with.

● KRISTEN, AGE 10

Q: What do you call a man with no shins?

A: Toe-knee.

● PAUL WALSH

Q: How do you sink a submarine full of idiots?

A: Knock on the door.

● DAMIAN SHORTEN

Q: What's round and bad-tempered?

A: A vicious circle.

● DEBBIE BRIDEN

Q: Who are the most decent people in the hospital?

A: The ultrasound people.

● COMEDIAN DAVID O'DOHERTY

Q: Why does Snoop Dogg carry an umbrella?

A: Fa drizzle.

● DAVID LOWENSTEIN

Q: What do you call a bear with no teeth?

A: A gummy bear.

● KYLE NEAGLE

Q: How many surrealists does it take to change a light bulb?

A: Two. One to hold the giraffe and the other to fill the bathtub with brightly colored machine tools.

● TERRY SANGSTER

Q: Why did the Pope cross the road?

A: He crosses everything.

● TOM FLITTER

Q: What did one DNA say to another DNA?

A: Do these genes make me look fat?

● GARRISON KEILLOR ON "PRARIE HOME COMPANION"

Q: How do you stop a snake from striking?

A: Pay it a livable wage.

● CINDY PARISEAU

Q: Why did the Siamese twins go to London?

A: So the other one could drive.

● BUDDY BOLTON ON WWW.COMICSTRIPLIVE.COM

Q: How is a cheap violin like a jury trial?

A: Everyone sighs with relief when the case is closed.

● EARLE HITCHNER

Q: How many politicians does it take to change a light bulb?

A: It depends on how many it took under the previous administration.

● MIGUEL GONZALAEZ SZAMOCKI

Q: What happened to the man who crossed the Alps with his elephants?

A: He got mountains that never forgot.

● PETER CROMPTON

Q: Why is it that batteries are better than men?

A: Because they, at least, have a positive side.

● UMA

Q: What's gray, has four legs and a trunk?
A: A mouse on vacation.

Q: Boy: Do you have a date for Valentine's Day?
A: Girl: Yes, February 14th.

Q: How far can a fox run into a grove?
A: Only halfway—then he's running out of it!

Q: I travel all over the world, but I always stay in my corner. What am I?
A: A stamp.

Q: What part of a fish weighs the most?
A: The scales.

Q: How many DIY buffs does it take to change a light bulb?
A: One, but it takes two weeks and four trips to the hardware store.

Q: Why wouldn't they let the butterfly into the dance?
A: Because it was a mothball.

Q: What's the difference between the government and the Mafia?
A: One of them is organized.

Q: What's worse than raining cats and dogs?
A: Hailing taxis.

Q: What's the difference between a dry cleaner and a lawyer?
A: The cleaner pays if he loses your suit. A lawyer can lose your suit and still take you to the cleaners.

Q: How do you get down from an elephant?
A: You don't. You get down from a goose.

I can't understand why a person will take a year to write a novel when he can easily buy one for a few dollars.

FRED ALLEN

Q: What's an astronaut's favorite key on the keyboard?

A: The spacebar.

● AKHIL GUPTA

Q: What did the scientist say to his stubborn, argumentative clone?

A: "Why can't you be a reasonable facsimile?"

● MARK SOLOMON

Q: What do you call someone who has just printed 1000 puns off the Internet?

A: Well e-quipped.

● J.C. PICKETT

Q: What's the best way to describe a bachelor?

A: A man who never Mrs. a woman.

● JANICE WILSON

Q: What do you get if you cross a monkey with an elephant?

A: Broken trees.

● JAMES FINDLAY

Q: Why do owls avoid kissing in the rain?

A: Because it's too wet to woo.

● RICHARD PADWELL

Q: How could the farmer be sure his honey was organic?

A: Because his bees had issued him with a swarm statement.

● WENDY AUSTIN

Q: What do elephants get for lunch at London Zoo?

A: Half an hour, the same as the penguins.

● JIM HANKINSON

If you arrest a mime, do you still have to tell him he has the right to remain silent?

Q: What happens if you play country music backwards?

A: You sober up, your estranged wife comes home and your faithful dog comes back to life.

● EDDIE LAMPTEY

Q: What did one plate say to the other plate?

A: Lunch is on me.

● ROBERT SHELLEY

Q: What do you call an overweight alien?

A: An extra-cholesterol.

● GRAHAM KENWARD

Q: Which Egyptian king used to loose his temper on the roads?

A: Toot-In-Car-Man

● JOHN HOODLESS

I saw a documentary on how ships are kept together; It was riveting.

STEWART FRANCIS

Q: A man is pushing his car along, and when he comes to a hotel he shouts, "I'm bankrupt!" Why?

A: He's playing Monopoly.

Q: This word I know? Six letters it contains. Take away the last. . . . and only twelve remains. What is the word?

A: "Dozens."

Q: I am the beginning of the end, and the end of time and space. I am essential to creation, and I surround every place. Who am I?

A: The letter E.

Q: Why was the goat excited?

A: Because there was a new 'kid' on the block.

Q: Why couldn't the octopus become a model?

A: Because it was all arms and no legs.

Q: Why does vegan cheese taste bad?

A: It hasn't been tested on mice.

Q: How many seconds are there in one year?

A: 12 of them: January 2nd, February 2nd, March 2nd, April 2nd, May 2nd, June 2nd, July 2nd, August 2nd, September 2nd, October 2nd, November 2nd, December 2nd.

Q: The man who made it doesn't want it. The man who bought it doesn't need it. The man who needs it doesn't know it. What am I talking about?

A: A coffin.

Q: Yellow I look and massive I weigh. In the morning I come to brighten your day. What am I?

A: A school bus.

Q: Why is the letter A the most like a flower?

A: Because the B is after it.

Q: What do you get if you cross Bambi with a ghost?

A: Bamboo.

● I. BELL

Q: What's the difference between a man and a municipal bond?

A: Municipal bonds will eventually mature.

● AGNES LANGER

Q: What do fishermen and hypochondriacs have in common?

A: They don't really have to catch anything to be happy.

● ROBERT ORBEN

Q: Why is psychoanalysis a lot quicker for men than for women?

A: When it's time to go back to his childhood, he's already there.

● MARTHA J. KIELEK

Q: What do you get if you cross a door-knocker with a zucchini?

A: Rat-a-tat-a-touille.

● MOLLIE BAXTER

Q: What do you call a judge with no thumbs?

A: Just his fingers.

● HITEN VADGAMA

Q: What do you get if you cross a snowman and a man-eating shark?

A: Frostbite.

● PAUL KEEL

I often wonder about people who live in tropical destinations. What do their screen savers look like?

"How can a cowardly lion cry?—How can a tin man talk?—How can a scarecrow dance?"

Q: What happens when a camera gets angry?
A: It snaps.

● ANOOP PARIHAR

Q: What's the best way to kill a circus?
A: Go for the juggler.

● GAIL CARDEW

Q: Which dogs do scientists like?
A: Lab-radors.

● MIMI LAMBA

Q: What's the true love of a sailor?

A: Fish and ships.

● GUNJAN RANA

Q: What's the difference between an elephant and a greyhound?

A: About 50 years' hard sandpapering.

● SINCLAIR TROTTER

Q: What does December have that other months don't have?

A: The letter D.

Q: What can run, but never walks? Has a mouth, but never talks? Has a head, but never weeps? Has a bed, but never sleeps?

A: A river.

Q: A man rode in to town on Tuesday, and left two days later on Tuesday. How so?

A: His horse is named Tuesday!

Q: What are two things you wouldn't eat after waking up?

A: Lunch and dinner.

Q: Why did the boy throw a bucket out the window?

A: He wanted to see the waterfall.

Q: Why did the boy throw butter out the window?

A: He wanted to see the butterfly.

Q: If a red-house is made of red bricks, has a red wooden door, and a red roof, and a yellow-house is made of yellow bricks, has a yellow wooden door, and a yellow roof, then what is a green-house made of?

A: Glass.

Q: What did one boat say to the other?

A: "Are you up for a little row-mance?"

Q: Why did the boy throw his watch out the window?

A: He wanted to see time fly.

Q: Why can't someone living in Maine be buried in Florida?

A: Because he's still living!

Q: What do pandas have that no other animal has?

A: Baby pandas!

Q: Which is the most curious letter?

A: Y?

Q: Which month has 28 days?

A: All of them, silly!

Q: What starts with a P, ends with an E, and has thousands of letters?

A: The Post Office!

Q: What kind of cheese is made backwards?

A: Edam.

Q: What word begins and ends with an E, but only has one letter?

A: Envelope!

Q: What five-letter word becomes shorter when you add two letters to it?

A: Short!

Q: Poor people have it. Rich people need it. If you eat it, you'll die. What is it?

A: Nothing!

Q: What do you throw out when you want to use it, but take in when you don't want to use it?

A: An anchor.

Q: Why do teachers consider themselves special?

A: Because they have a class of their own.

● AMIT BARTAKE

Q: I have a head but no body, a heart but no blood. Just leaves and no branches, I grow without wood. What am I?

A: Lettuce!

Q: Why do hummingbirds hum?

A: Because they can't remember the words.

Q: What only gets wetter the more it dries?

A: A towel!

Q: What is easy to get into, but hard to get out of?

A: Trouble.

Q: How do you keep cool at a football game?

A: Stand next to a fan.

Q: Why did the football coach go to the bank?

A: To get his quarterback.

Q: How many college football players does it take to change a lightbulb?

A: The entire team. And they each get a semester's credit for it.

Q: What do you call a pig that does karate?

A: A pork chop.

Q: What did Adam say the day before Christmas?

A: It's Christmas, Eve!

I haven't slept for ten days, because that would be too long.

● MITCH HEDBERG

Q: What do you get when you combine a Christmas tree with an iPad?

A: A pineapple.

Q: What did the reindeer say before telling his joke?

A: This one'll sleigh you!

Q: What do you say to your single friends on Valentine's Day?

A: Happy Independence Day!

HOLIDAY
FUNNIES

> **"** I've just been on a once-in-a-lifetime holiday. I'll tell you what—NEVER AGAIN. **"**
>
> TIM VINE

'TIS **THE SEASON**

I had finished my Christmas shopping early and had wrapped all the presents. Having two curious children, I had to find a suitable hiding place. I chose an ideal spot—the furnace room. I stacked the presents and covered them with a blanket, positive they'd remain undiscovered.

When I went to get the gifts to put them under the tree, I lifted the blanket and there, stacked neatly on top of my gifts, were presents addressed to "Mom and Dad, From the Kids."

● LORALIE LONG

A teenager waltzed into our jewelry store to buy a cross for her boyfriend. I showed her a selection, and she pointed to three: "Can I see that one, that one, and the one with the little man on it?"

"Oh," I replied. "You mean Jesus?"

● JULIE SWARSBRICK

In the old days, it was not called the Holiday Season; the Christians called it "Christmas" and went to church; the Jews called it "Hanukkah" and went to synagogue; the atheists went to parties and drank. People passing each other on the street would say "Merry Christmas!" or "Happy Hanukkah!" or (to the atheists) "Look out for the wall!"

● DAVE BARRY

From an article on the Woolacombe Bay Hotel in Devon, England: "Their three-night Christmas break includes a packed program of family entertainment, a crèche, excellent cuisine, and a visit from Satan."

"Shoot . . . I brought my garbage by mistake."

Did you hear that Rudolph the Red-Nosed Reindeer never went to school? That's right—he was elf taught.

This past Christmas, I told my girlfriend that all I wanted was an Xbox. That's it. Beginning and end of list: Xbox. You know what she got me? A homemade frame with a picture of us from our first date together. Which was fine. Because I got her an Xbox.

● ANTHONY JESELNIK

Michel and I were newlyweds living in a small apartment. Just before Christmas, my parents came to dinner and asked us what gifts we'd like.

"I'd love a puppy!" I blurted out.

"All right," Michel agreed, "provided he remains small, doesn't bark, makes no fuss, stays clean and is no trouble."

"I think I know just the breed for you," my father said, smiling.

In the days that followed, Michel and I tried to guess what it would be. Maybe a Yorkshire Terrier or a Dachshund—they're small. Or one of those placid, undemanding Italian Toy Grayhounds.

Christmas Eve arrived at last, and my father proudly presented us with a pretty wicker basket that we opened excitedly. Inside was an adorable little dog—a stuffed one.

● MARIE-PIERRE PIAT

When our son Patrick was four, we still marked all his Christmas presents "From Santa Claus." A couple of hours after they had been opened on Christmas Day, I noticed that he seemed quite glum, for no apparent reason. "What was the matter?"

"Well," said Patrick. Long pause. "Well, I, I really thought you and mommy would give me something for Christmas."

● ALEXANDER FARRELL

A mother gave her grown son two sweaters for Hanukkah. The next time he visited, he made sure to wear one. As he entered her home, instead of the expected smile, she frowned. "What's the matter?" she asked. "You didn't like the other one?"

● JENNIFER PAULY

My daughter Aurore had just written a huge list of presents, and her mother was trying to explain that Father Christmas wouldn't be able to bring them all.

"Oh, that doesn't matter," shurgged Aurore, "You can buy the rest."

● PATRICE BERNARD

Last Christmas, after midnight mass, the whole family got together around a table groaning with goodies, in a very friendly atmosphere. Just for fun in the course of the conversation, the grownups asked the children what they wanted to be when they grew up. My little nephew, age six, replied without hesitation, "I want to be a priest!"

Everybody oohed and aahed in admiration of this precocious calling. The child's grandmother, very moved, asked, "And why do you want to be a priest, darling?"

"To get the money from the collection!"

Everybody fell silent, and the subject never came up again.

● MONSIEUR HAUBERT

My parents were kind of over protective people. Me and my sister had to play in the backyard all the time. They bought us bikes for Christmas but wouldn't let us ride in the street, we had to ride in the backyard. Another Christmas, my dad got me a basketball hoop and put it in the middle of the lawn! You can't dribble on grass.

● JIMMY FALLON

My family wasn't very religious; on Hanukkah, they had a menorah on a dimmer.

● RICHARD LEWIS

EASTER BONNETS

My sister was busy getting ready to host our entire family for Easter. On her to-do list was a hair appointment for her daughter. "So, Katie," said the stylist as the little girl got up in the chair, "who's coming to your house this weekend with big ears and floppy feet?"

Katie replied, "I think it's my uncle Brian."

● MARASHA ECKERMAN

The subject line on the e-mail sent by our campus ministry after Easter read "He is risen!" But the next day, we received a rather startling message intended to clear up a minor typo in the first e-mail.

The subject line now read "He is risen—correction."

● SETH BREUNIG

He was doomed to fail, but last Easter, my husband tried unsuccessfully to get our young sons to have some lunch after they'd already stuffed themselves with a ton of chocolate eggs.

"They're not going to eat," my mother-in-law told him. "It's Easter Sunday. What do you expect, a miracle?"

● JENNIFER SMITH

At an Easter-week meeting of Weight Watchers, a woman said proudly this was the first year her children realized that chocolate Easter bunnies came with ears.

● DEBRA SCHNEIDER

"What kind of parents let their children get tattoos?"

Last Easter, my youngest daughter's daycare teacher gave each of her pupils a little basket of chocolates carefully wrapped in cellophane. Before we were even out of the daycare center, I saw Jade—who was four at the time—trying to open the much-desired package.

"Didn't Chantal tell you not to eat them until you got home?"

"Yes, she did," said Jade, "but I didn't hear her."

● MARIE-PIERRE AUCLAIR

I must admit, I looked forward to our upcoming church service with greater anticipation than usual after reading in our bulletin, "This being Easter Sunday, we will ask Mrs. Brown to come forward and lay an egg on the altar."

● MAUREEN BENCZE

When he was a child, my son was a poor eater. On Good Friday, at my parish church hall they were going to show a movie for the children. I promised my son that if he ate well that week I would take him to see the movie.

I took him as promised, but first I went into the church to pray. As it was near Easter, there were lots of people milling around the confession boxes. My son looked around with astonishment on his face and then smiled and said: "Mom, this movie must be really great. Just look at how many people there are at the ticket offices!"

● MARIA CECÍLIA FONSECA

LUCK O' THE **IRISH**

An Irishman proposes to his girl on St. Patrick's Day and gave her a ring with a synthetic diamond.

On learning it wasn't real, she protested vehemently about his cheapness.

"It was in honor of St. Patrick's Day," he smiled. "I gave you a sham-rock."

● HAROLD EMERY

After a leisurely soak in a friend's hot tub, I found that a chemical reaction had turned my long, bleached hair bright green from the middle of my head down. Unable to do anything about it that afternoon, I twisted my green locks into a chignon and went off to work. To my surprise, I made triple my usual tips waiting on tables. I had forgotten that it was March 17—St. Patrick's Day.

● PATRICIA R. STONSBY

> If a man who cannot count finds a four-leaf clover, is he lucky?
>
> STANISLAW J. LEC

For our church's ladies' fellowship night in March, we decided to have a St. Patrick's Day theme and wear something green. Each lady who did would receive a small gift. With all the changes in making up the invitation, the printed message finally read: each lady wearing something will receive a gift.

● KAREN LINDSTROM

On St. Patrick's Day, most of the men in my office wear a spot of green. Usually the color appears in a conservative necktie. At our coffee break, we were admiring the various shades of green displayed by the secretaries when we were joined by Jose, a fellow engineer. Jose is a Mexican-American, and proud of it. Nevertheless, he too was wearing the green. Pinned to his jacket was a plump and glossy green chili pepper!

● JOHN W. TORRANCE

How can you tell if a leprechaun is having a good time? He is Dublin over with laughter!

TURKEY TIME

During Thanksgiving dinner last year, my eight-year-old son watched intently as my husband carved the turkey. "Man," he said in awe. "They must have fed bread to that turkey for months to get all that stuffing."

● HEATHER JOHNSON

"I always thought 'Giblets' was a really funny word, too, until I Googled it!"

Before Thanksgiving a Minnesota first-grade teacher asked her pupils to tell her what they had to be thankful for. "I am thankful," said one small boy, "that I am not a turkey."

"If you wish to make an apple pie truly from scratch you must first invent the universe."

● CARL SAGAN

When a Butterball Talk-Line staffer asked a caller what state her turkey was in (meaning how thawed was it) the caller responded with, "Florida."

● SOURCE: BUTTERBALL TURKEY TALK-LINE

"Cooking Tip: Wrap turkey leftovers in aluminum foil and throw them out."

● NICOLE HOLLANDER

An optimist is anyone who has a 28-pound turkey for Thanksgiving and the next day asks, "What's for lunch?"

"If you want to save a species, simply decide to eat it. Then it will be managed—like chickens, like turkeys, like deer, like Canadian geese."

● TED NUGENT

My cooking is so bad my kids thought Thanksgiving was to commemorate Pearl Harbor.

● PHYLLIS DILLER

" I come from a family where gravy is considered a beverage."

● ERMA BOMBECK

A disappointed woman called Butterball's Thanksgiving Turkey Talk-Line wondering why her turkey had no breast meat. After a conversation with an operator, it became apparent that the woman's turkey was lying on the table upside down.

● SOURCE: BUTTERBALL TURKEY TALK-LINE

" Thanksgiving dinners take 18 hours to prepare. They are consumed in 12 minutes. Half-times take 12 minutes. This is not coincidence."

● ERMA BOMBECK

" Vegetables are a must on a diet. I suggest carrot cake, zucchini bread, and pumpkin pie.

● JIM DAVIS

GOBLINS, GHOULS **AND GHOSTS**

My six-year-old son was excited about his Halloween costume. "I'm going to be the Pope," he said.

"Ian, you can't be the Pope," I said. "You're not Catholic. You're Lutheran."

Ian hadn't thought about that. So he considered his alternatives. After a few minutes, he asked, "Is Dracula a Lutheran?"

● JENNY CRANE

This Halloween the most popular mask is the Arnold Schwarzenegger mask. And the best part? With a mouth full of candy you will sound just like him.

● CONAN O'BRIEN

For Halloween my children and I decorated the small area inside our front door with spiders and webs, ghosts, skeletons, a severed arm, floating eyeballs, fog and horror music. We were dressed in our witch and ghoul costumes to greet the trick-or-treaters. My son's teen-age friends were impressed with our efforts. We were worried, however, about frightening the youngsters. But one costumed tot pushed through the group at the door, left his treat bag on the doorstep, stepped inside and asked, "Can I look at the rest of your house too?"

● MARION MCKEAND-CLEMENT

After giving it a lot of thought, my son announced that he considered Halloween a far better holiday than Easter.
"Why's that?" my husband asked.
"Because," he said, "on Halloween, I'm given candy. Easter, I have to find it."

● DEANE BRUMFIELD

One Halloween, I ran out of treats for the children but kept the lights on and answered the door. When two boys arrived, I told them I didn't have anything left. One lad said, "not even a chocolate bar for yourself?" No, not a single one. He took a bar out of his bag and and said, "here, have one of mine."

● ELLEN STONE

I asked the three children I babysit what they had dressed up as for Halloween the rainy night before.

"Emily was a princess," four-year-old William said, "and I was a baseball player."

I asked what two-year-old Jacob's costume had been. "Jacob was a raincoat."

● KATRINA RATZ

After the Halloween rush at my parents' costume business, we discovered that we had many clown noses left unsold. My mom decided to set up a sale box on the counter, hoping they'd move a little faster. And they did, after she put a sign over the box that read: "Pick your nose here!"

● PAULINE KINGSMAN

My sister decided to have a Halloween makeup booth at the local mall, but couldn't think of a catchy name for it. However, when the day arrived and I was helping her set up, she handed me a bowl of candy kisses and a banner that read: KISS AND MAKE UP.

● MARILYN HEAD

Last Halloween I opened the door to three sheet-festooned figures of varying heights. "Trick or treat," they chorused in unison.

Having had a bad day, I gave the trio a stern lecture on moral blackmail. I finished my tirade by demanding, "And what was your trick going to be?"

The smallest replied with a squeak, "I was going to say 'Boo!'" They got their treat.

● JEAN GIBS

"You trick or treated the neighborhoods . . .
I hit the banks."

At the pharmacy where I work, we wear a costume on Halloween. I once dressed up as a clown and wore a red foam ball on my nose. But the nose kept falling off, and it finally happened when I was serving a customer. As we watched it roll across the floor, the customer quipped, "Boy, that sure is a runny nose."

● EILEEN TKACHYK

As we went from door to door on Halloween night, people always commented on my three sons' costumes. "You're the Black Knight," they said to nine-year-old Tyler, wearing his chain mail, sword and breastplate; "And you're Dracula," to my youngest son, six-year-old Cole; and to my middle son, Nelson, dressed in his toga and vine-leaf wreath, they said, "You must be Caesar."

"No," he corrected, "I'm Zeus."

After this happened a number of times, Cole said, "People think Nelson's a salad cause you made him wear those leaves on his head."

● BONITA SIEGEL

Halloween evening I was happily handing out treats to the little "witches" and "goblins" of our neighborhood. Having given out chocolate bars to a couple of boys, I noticed I had many candy kisses left, so as they hurried across the yard I called, "Oh, I should have given you some kisses, too!"

One little fellow stopped, looked back and answered, "I like candy better."

● ADELA BERSTAD

On Halloween night, my five-year-old daughter hesitated on the front walk of one home—a man was sitting on the porch dressed up like an ogre. Just then a woman came outside with a cup of coffee. Laura happily ran up their walk, calling back to me, "It's okay, Mom, he has a mother."

● JANINE MAXWELL

Halloween is a big event in the neighborhood we had moved to—decorations, haunted houses, and several homeowners even dressed up in costumes. One woman who answered the door to my children was in a gaudy dress, garish makeup and a wild hairdo. We commented on her costume while the kids received their candy.

A month later I bumped into the same lady at the grocery store. Imagine my embarrassment when it registered—she hadn't changed a bit!

● L. ALLIN CANNADY

On Halloween, I opened the door to a child no more than four years old. As I held out the candy dish, our dog Samy came up to her, barking joyously.

"You have a dog?" said the little girl, surprised.

I told her that Samy likes children and would not hurt her. Still, she stepped back.

"Yes," she said, not reassured, "but I'm dressed as a cat!"

● MARTINE L. GONTHIER

As a school-bus driver I wear a costume on Halloween. Last year I was a scarecrow, complete with straw hair. After my day at work, I drove my two youngest kids to Grandma's house to show her our costumes. To avoid the trick-or-treaters, I took an alternate route, and five-year-old Tyler asked repeatedly if I was lost. I assured him that I'd driven to Grandma's hundreds of times.

"Oh," Tyler replied. "Well, I wasn't sure, because we all know that scarecrows only have straw for brains."

● CYNDY HESLIN

One evening in mid-October last year, I answered a knock on the door. There in front of me was a tall youth with a Dracula mask on his head. "Trick or treat," he announced.

I complimented him on his scary appearance but told him that Halloween was not for another two weeks.

"I know," he replied. "But I'm away then."

● JIM ROBERTSON

I went to a Halloween party where everyone was in costume, except for this one fellow who was dressed handsomely and was carting around a long piece of lumber that looked like a 2 x 4. I stopped trying to guess what his costume was, and instead just asked what he was dressed as. He pointed to himself and the piece of wood and said, "We're a couple of studs."

● MICHELE COUTU

HEARTS AND FLOWERS

During World War II my parents had planned a romantic Valentine's Day wedding. Suddenly my father, then stationed at Camp Edwards in Massachusetts, received orders to prepare to ship out, and all leaves were canceled. Being a young man in love, he went AWOL. He and my mother were married four days earlier than originally planned and he returned to base to an angry sergeant. After hearing the explanation, the sergeant understandingly replied, "Okay, okay!" Then, as an afterthought: "But don't let it happen again!"

● SANDRA L. CARON

My husband, a certified public accountant, works 15-hour days for the first few months of the year. In spite of his hectic schedule, he took time out to order me flowers for Valentine's Day. While pondering what sweet endearment to write on the card, he obviously began thinking of the many hours of work still ahead of him. His note read: "Roses are red, violets are blue. If I weren't thinking of you, I'd probably be through."

● CINDY WOLF

What did the chef give his wife on Valentine's Day? A hug and a quiche.

● JOHN SIERZANT

My friend Mark and I work in a lawn-mower-parts warehouse. Somehow Mark got the idea that his wife did not want a card on Valentine's Day, but when he spoke to her on the phone he discovered she was expecting one. Not having time to buy a card on his way home, Mark was in a quandary. Then he looked at the lawn-mower trade magazines scattered around the office—and got an idea. Using scissors and glue, he created a card with pictures of mowers, next to which he wrote: "I lawn for you mower and mower each day."

● GENE HYDE

I don't know why Cupid was chosen to represent Valentine's Day. When I think about romance, the last thing on my mind is a short, chubby toddler coming at me with a weapon.

● COMIC PAUL MCGINTY

"It's Valentine's Day and you couldn't even get me a card?"

Every Valentine's Day our campus newspaper has a section for student messages. Last year my roommate surprised his girlfriend with roses and dinner at a fancy restaurant. When they returned from their date, she leafed through the paper to see if he had written a note to her. Near the bottom of one page she found: "Bonnie—What are you looking here for? Aren't dinner and flowers enough? Love, Scott."

● RICHARD B. BLACKWELL

It was Valentine's Day and my three-and-a-half-year-old daughter, Kimberly, and I decided we would surprise my husband with a special dinner. We shopped for the ingredients and I prepared his favorite meal. Then we set the table with our best tablecloth, china, crystal and candles. At the last moment, we decided we should dress up for this special event. We ran to our bedrooms. I donned my black cocktail dress and then met Kimberly in the hall, wearing her Halloween bunny costume.

● JANICE STARYK

As Valentine's Day approached, I tried to think of an unusual gift for my husband. When I discovered that his favorite red-plaid pants had a broken zipper, I thought I had the "perfect Valentine." I had the pants repaired, and gift-wrapped them. On the package I put a huge red heart on which I printed: "My Heart Pants for You." I was the surprised one, however, when I saw the same heart taped to our formerly empty, but now overflowing, wood box. On it he had written: "Wood You Be My Valentine?"

● MARY LOU PITTMAN

My high-school English teacher was well known for being a fair, but hard, grader. One day I received a B minus on a theme paper. In hopes of bettering my grade and in the spirit of the Valentine season, I sent her an extravagant heart-shaped box of chocolates with the pre-printed inscription: "BE MINE."

The following day, I received in return a valentine from the teacher. It read: "Thank you, but it's still BE MINE-US."

● BRAD WILCOX

The lingerie store where my aunt works was crowded with shoppers selecting Valentine's Day gifts for their wives. A young businessman came to the register with a lacy black negligee. My aunt noticed that the next customer, an elderly farmer, was holding a long flannel nightgown and kept glancing at the younger man's sexier choice. When it was his turn, the farmer placed the nightgown on the counter. "Would you have anything in black flannel?" he asked.

● CHRISTINE A. PANDOLFO

In fourth grade, my son had a huge crush on a classmate. So for Valentine's Day, he bought her a box of chocolates and took it into school. When I returned home from work, I found him on the couch eating the same box of candy.

"What happened?" I asked.

"Well, I thought about it for a long time," he said between chews.

"And I decided that, for now, I still like candy more than girls."

● KYM LOKKEN

KNOCK! KNOCK! WHO'S THERE?

" I always wanted to be somebody, but I guess I should've been more specific. **"**

LILY TOMLIN

KNOCK! KNOCK!
Who's there?
Justin.
Justin who?
Justin the neighborhood and thought I'd come over.

KNOCK! KNOCK!
Who's there?
Isabelle.
Isabelle who?
Isabelle working, or should I keep knocking?

KNOCK! KNOCK!
Who's there?
Ya.
Ya who?
I'm excited to see you too!

KNOCK! KNOCK!
Who's there?
Boo hoo.
Boo hoo who?
Aww, don't cry—it's just a joke.

● AUDREY DEE

KNOCK! KNOCK!
Who's there?
H.
H who?
Bless you!

● HEIDI HOFBAUER-WAGNITZ

KNOCK! KNOCK!
Who's there?
Alpaca.
Alpaca who?
Alpaca the trunk, you pack up the suitcase.

● LYN PARKER

PRIMITIVE MAN DISCOVERS COMEDY

KNOCK! KNOCK!
Who's there?
Witches.
Witches who?
Witches the way home?

● CAROLINE JOYCE

KNOCK! KNOCK!
Who's there?
Sam and Janet.
Sam and Janet who?
Samenjanet Evening.

● VICKI STEPHENS

KNOCK! KNOCK!
Who's there?
Goat.
Goat who?
Goat to the door to see who's knocking!

● AUDREY DEE

KNOCK! KNOCK!
Who's there?
Cash.
Cash who?
I didn't realize you were some kind of nut!

● LATASHA ROBINSON

KNOCK! KNOCK!
Who's there?
Harry.
Harry who?
Harry up and let me in!

KNOCK! KNOCK!
Who's there?
Dozen.
Dozen who?
Dozen anyone want to let me in?

KNOCK! KNOCK!
Who's there?
Dishes.
Dishes who?
Dishes a nice place you got here.

KNOCK! KNOCK!
Who's there?
Control freak—now you say, "Control freak who?"

KNOCK! KNOCK!
Who's there?
Claire.
Claire who?
Claire the way; I'm coming in!

KNOCK! KNOCK!
Who's there?
Canoe.
Canoe who?
Canoe open the door?

KNOCK! KNOCK!
Who's there?
Ben.
Ben who?
Ben knocking for 20 minutes!

KNOCK! KNOCK!
Who's there?
Orange.
Orange who?
Orange you gonna open the door?

● CAROLINE JOYCE

KNOCK! KNOCK!
Who's there?
Amos.
Amos who?
A mosquito bit me!

● LAURIE CALLIER

KNOCK! KNOCK!
Who's there?
Weevil.
Weevil who?
Weevil weevil rock you.

● LUBNA WALI

> You can't knock on opportunity's door and not be ready.
>
> BRUNO MARS

"You're knock, knock jokes aren't funny. They stink!"

KNOCK! KNOCK!
Who's there?
Howl.
Howl who?
Howl you know it's really me unless you open the door?

KNOCK! KNOCK!
Who's there?
Heidi.
Heidi who?
Heidi 'cided to come over to play!

KNOCK! KNOCK.
Who's there?
To.
To who?
No, to whom.

KNOCK! KNOCK!
Who's there?
Keith!
Keith who?
Keith me, thweet heart!

KNOCK! KNOCK!
Who's there?
Radio.
Radio who?
Radio not, here I come!

● DIANE PAGE

KNOCK! KNOCK!
Who's there?
Robin.
Robin who?
Robin' you! So hand over your money!

● SYEDA MANSURA BANU

A man entered the local paper's pun contest. He sent in ten different entries, hoping that at least one of them would win. Unfortunately, no pun in ten did.

KNOCK! KNOCK!
Who's there?
Broken pencil.
Broken pencil who?
Forget it—this joke is pointless.

KNOCK! KNOCK!
Who's there?
Ken.
Ken who?
Ken you let me in?

KNOCK! KNOCK!
Who's there?
Will.
Will who?
Will you just open the door already?

KNOCK! KNOCK!
Who's there?
Ice cream.
Ice cream who?
ICE CREAM RIGHT NOW IF YOU DON'T LET ME IN!

KNOCK! KNOCK!
Who's there?
Ketchup.
Ketchup who?
Ketchup with me and I'll tell you!

● CATHERINE WILCOX

KNOCK! KNOCK!
Who's there?
Chester and Ima.
Chester and Ima who?
Chester minute. Ima Busy!

● BARBARA RANKIN

KNOCK! KNOCK!
Who's there?
Figs.
Figs who?
Figs your doorbell, it's not working!

KNOCK! KNOCK!
Who's there?
Alex.
Alex who?
Hey, Alex the questions around here!

KNOCK! KNOCK!
Who's there?
A little old lady.
A little old lady who?
I didn't know you could yodel!

KNOCK! KNOCK!
Who's there?
Wendy.
Wendy who?
Wendy bell works again I won't have to knock anymore.

KNOCK! KNOCK!
Who's there?
Annie.
Annie who?
Annie body going to open the door already?

KNOCK! KNOCK!
Who's there?
Noah.
Noah who?
Noah any place I can get a bite to eat?

KNOCK! KNOCK!
Who's there?
Ho-ho.
Ho-ho who?
You know, your Santa impression could use a little work.

KNOCK! KNOCK!
Who's there?
Somebody.
Somebody who?
Somebody who can't reach the doorbell!

KNOCK! KNOCK!
Who's there?
Doris.
Doris who?
Doris locked. Open up!

KNOCK! KNOCK!
Who's there?
Tank.
Tank who?
You're welcome!

KNOCK! KNOCK!
Who's there?
Lettuce.
Lettuce who?
Lettuce in already!

KNOCK! KNOCK!
Who's there?
Olive.
Olive who?
Olive you and I don't care who knows it.

KNOCK! KNOCK!
Who's there?
Luke.
Luke who?
Luke through the keyhole to see!

KNOCK! KNOCK!
Who's there?
Needle.
Needle who?
Needle little help gettin' in the door.

KNOCK! KNOCK!
Who's there?
Hanna.
Hanna who?
. . . Hanna partridge in a pear tree!

KNOCK! KNOCK!
Who's there?
Mary and Abbey.
Mary and Abbey who?
Mary Christmas and Abbey New Year!

KNOCK! KNOCK!
Who's there?
Irish.
Irish who?
Irish you a Merry Christmas!

KNOCK! KNOCK!
Who's there?
Santa.
Santa who?
Santa email reminding you I'd be here, and you
   STILL make me wait in the cold!

KNOCK! KNOCK!
Who's there?
Yule log.
Yule log who?
Yule log the door after you let me in, won't you?

*Sitting at a stoplight, I was puzzling over the
meaning of the vanity plate on the car in front of
me. It read "Innie." Then I got it. The make of the car
was Audi.*

● **KATHY JOHNSON**

KNOCK! KNOCK!
Who's there?
Snow.
Snow who?
Snow use. I forgot my name again!

KNOCK! KNOCK!
Who's there?
Carmen.
Carmen who?
Carmen let me in already!

KNOCK! KNOCK!
Who's there?
Convex.
Convex who?
Convex go to prison!

KNOCK! KNOCK!
Who's there?
Sherlock.
Sherlock who?
Sherlock your door shut tight.

KNOCK! KNOCK!
Who's there?
Scold.
Scold who?
Scold outside—let me in!

KNOCK! KNOCK!
Who's there?
Police.
Police who?
Police hurry—I'm freezing out here!

> Puns are a form of humor with words.
>
> GUILLERMO CABRERA INFANTE

KNOCK! KNOCK!

Who's there?

Otto.

Otto who?

Otto know what's taking you so long!

KNOCK! KNOCK!

Who's there?

Ach.

Ach who?

Bless you!

KNOCK! KNOCK!

Who's there?

The interrupting cow.

The interr . . .

MOOOOO!

KNOCK! KNOCK!

Who's there?

Aida.

Aida who?

Aida lot of sweets and now I've got a tummy ache!

KNOCK! KNOCK!

Who's there?

Wanda.

Wanda who?

Wanda hang out with me right now?

KIDS SAY
THE DARNDEST THINGS

" When I was a child my father attacked me with cameras; I still have flashbacks. "

STEWART FRANCIS

"Yaawn. My imaginary friend kept me
up late last night."

OUT OF THE **MOUTHS OF BABES**

En route to church to make his first confession, my nervous seven-year-old grandson asked me what he could expect.

"Confession is where you tell all the bad things you've done to the priest," I told him.

He looked relieved. "Good. I haven't done anything bad to the priest."

● DOUGLAS MATOOK

In the British documentary *56 Up,* a man shared that he had earned a law degree at Oxford. Then, in his thick English accent, he proudly proclaimed that he was now a "barrister."

My thirteen-year-old daughter wasn't impressed. "So," she said, "he spent all that effort getting an Oxford law degree, and now he works at Starbucks?"

● LAUREN JOYCE

On Sam's eighth birthday, my brother took him to a football game. During halftime, a Marine band played, and Sam studied them intently.

"Why the interest in the band?" his father asked.

"I'm checking to see if Ben and Matt from our synagogue are in it. They're Marines."

"But they're in Afghanistan."

"If I were in a marching band, I'd say I was in Afghanistan too."

● CHANA PAWLIGER

As I was nursing my baby, my cousin's six-year-old daughter, Krissy, came into the room. Never having seen anyone breast-feed before, she was intrigued and full of all kinds of questions about what I was doing.

After mulling over my answers, she remarked, "My mom has some of those, but I don't think she knows how to use them."

● LOIS SINGER

I was telling my three boys the story of the Nativity and how the Wise Men brought gifts of gold, frankincense and myrrh for the infant Jesus.

Clearly giving it a lot of thought, my six-year-old observed, "Mom, a Wise Woman would have brought diapers."

● ANGIE FLAUTE

When my eight-year-old sister came to visit, I took a day off from my job at the Pentagon and showed her the Lincoln Memorial. There she saw a large block of text—273 words long—etched into the monument.

"What's that?" she asked.

"Lincoln's Gettysburg Address," I told her.

"If that's his address, how does he get any mail?"

● DANIEL PALOMO

I overheard my seven-year-old son and his friends discussing the Tooth Fairy, Easter Bunny and Santa Claus.

"Steven says it's the parents who bring the toys," he said skeptically, "but I know my parents wouldn't know how to drive the reindeer."

● SHARON PRICE

After cleaning my five-year-old patient's teeth, I accompanied him to the reception area, only to see him struggle with the oak door.

"It's heavy, isn't it?" I asked.

"Yes," he said. "Is that so children can't escape?"

● JENNIFER SLOETJES

I picked up my nine-year-old daughter from school and asked how her day had gone. A few minutes later, I repeated the question, and again a few minutes after that. Instead of annoyed, Ariana was philosophical.

"Mom," she said, "your amnesia is my déjà vu."

● CLAIRE APONTE

GENERATION **GAP**

My husband, Garth, loves taking the kids out on Halloween. One year, he decided to start charging them a "daddy tax" on their candy. They each were to give him a small portion of the treats they received.

Halloween was coming up again, and the boys started saying, "How about if we don't have the daddy tax this year?"

"Yeah," they all said. "No daddy tax this year!"

"We're going to boycott the tax this year!" the boys said.

My four-year old, Celeste, added, "Yeah! And I'm going to girlcott it!"

● JANET SWANSON

Her class assignment was to interview an "old person" about his life, so my niece asked me, "What was the biggest historical event that happened during your childhood?"

"I'd have to say the moonwalk," I replied.

She looked disappointed. "That dance was so important to you?"

● JEAN ROSENSTEIL

I took my eight-year-old nephew, Kerry, to an Easter church service. When the collection plate came by, Kerry added his offering and I added mine.

Then Kerry leaned close and commented, "You'd think God would have enough money by now."

● JOHN LOUMP

On a demographics survey given at our high school, students were asked, "What disadvantages do you see in having children?" Usual answers included "It's expensive to raise kids," and "They take up a lot of your time."

But one boy was not worried about money or responsibility. He wrote, "If I have children, I might have to drive a minivan."

● CHERITH DIEMERT

I should have known better than to take my four-year-old son shopping with me. I spent the entire time in the mall chasing after him. Finally, I'd had it. "Do you want a stranger to take you?!" I scolded.

Thrilled, he yelled back, "Will he take me to the zoo?"

● KARLA PETERSILKA

"You're not going to look good in the 'How I Spent My Summer Vacation' essay."

After my ten-year-old daughter declared her disgust with cosmetic surgery, I dropped a bomb on her. "Don't be too quick to judge," I told her. "Before college, I had a nose job."

She was completely thrown. "You mean," she said, "it was bigger?"

● TANYA SCHERSCHEL

My mother was away all weekend at a business conference. During a break, she decided to call home collect. My six-year-old brother picked up the phone and heard a stranger's voice say, "We have a Marcia on the line. Will you accept the charges?"

Frantic, he dropped the receiver and came charging outside screaming, "Dad! They've got Mom! And they want money!"

● RODNEY HOWELL

A young boy was lost in the mall. He ran over to a police officer. "I've lost my dad!" he said.

"What's he like?" the cop asked.

"Baseball and beer."

Though the vocabulary words we were learning in my second-grade class sort of sounded the same, they had very different meanings.

This concept was not lost on one bright boy who knew what those differences were: "When people marry more than once, it's called polygamy. But when people marry only once, it's called monotony."

● RABIA FIDA

Our elementary school was honoring local veterans. The students were a bit intimidated and didn't know how to approach them.

"Start by introducing yourself," I said. "Then ask what branch of the military they served in."

One student walked over to a vet and promptly asked, "What tree are you from?"

● LISA WATERMAN

Studying our wedding photos, my six-year-old asked, "Did you marry Dad because he was good-looking?"

"Not really," I replied.

"Did you marry him for his money?"

"Definitely not," I laughed. "He didn't have any."

"So," he said, "you just felt sorry for him."

● LINDA WATSON

At my ten-year-old's request, I loaded my Rolling Stones tunes onto his iPod.

"I had no idea you liked the Stones," I said.

"Sure. I like all that old-fashioned music," he said.

"What do you mean, 'old-fashioned music'?"

"You know," he said defensively. "Music from the 1900s."

● MEG DIETRICH

Our three-year-old daughter was making up a poem when she asked us what rhymed with stop.

My husband said, "Think of something that's cool and refreshing but that Mom and I don't let you drink."

Our daughter knew the answer: "Alcohol!"

● JUDY BERKSETH

Do you know what you call those who use towels and never wash them, eat meals and never do the dishes, sit in rooms they never clean, and are entertained till they drop? If you have just answered, "A house guest," you're wrong because I have just described my kids.

● ERMA BOMBECK

"I'm considering a run for class president.
Do we have any skeletons in our closet I should
know about?"

My thirteen-year-old nephew thought his "gangsta" outfit—low-riding pants and exposed boxers—made him look cool. That is, until the day his five-year-old cousin took notice. "Nathaniel," she yelled out in front of everyone. "Your panties are showing."

● LINDA MCLEMORE

Our six-year-old daughter, Terra, has a need to ask questions . . . lots of questions. Finally, one day, my wife had had it.

"Have you ever heard that curiosity killed the cat?" my wife asked.

"No," replied Terra.

"Well, there was a cat, and he was very inquisitive. And one day, he looked into a big hole, fell in, and died!"

Terra was intrigued: "What was in the hole?"

● HECTOR BERNASCONI

"Where is Pearl Harbor?" I asked my fourth-grade history class. "Here's a hint: It's a place where everyone wants to go."

One student blurted out, "Candy Land!"

● KARA SILVER

My two sons, Jake and Austin, are a handful. So I wasn't surprised that Dad looked frazzled after we took them to a football game.

"It will be a cold day in #@%* before we come to another game," he muttered.

"Did you hear that?" Jake shouted to Austin. "Grandpa's going to take us to a game in December!"

● DREW SPECHT

While my three-year-old grandson was attending a birthday party, his friend's father sneaked off to take a shower before work. Halfway through, the father heard a tapping on the shower door, followed by the sight of my grandson peering in. Looking around the stall, he asked, "Is my mom in here?"

● BILLIE CREEL

My sister got a call from her son's kindergarten teacher. When he'd gone in to check on little James in the bathroom, he noticed the boy was using a urinal. "That's odd," my sister said. "We never taught him how to use a urinal."

"I could tell," said the teacher. "He was sitting in it."

● ESTHER OLCHEWSKI

Up on the screen at our local multiplex, the star whispered to his female costar, "I want you to be my mistress."

"What's a mistress?" my eight-year-old granddaughter yelled out.

Then the man gave the woman a passionate kiss.

"Never mind," my granddaughter said.

● LOIS WILKINS

"Daddy," said my eleven-year-old daughter, "I think I want to join the Army."

"Baby," I answered, "I think the Air Force would be a better option for you."

"But I don't want to be a pilot."

"You don't have to be a pilot," I told her. "There are other jobs in the Air Force."

Her answer: "I don't want to be a flight attendant either."

● RICHARD STEELE

Any kid will run an errand for you if you ask at bedtime.

● RED SKELTON

My mother taught for eleven years at a day-care center. One winter afternoon she was trying to show a young boy how to zip up his coat. "The secret," Mom said, "is to get this piece of the zipper to fit in the other side before you try to zip it up."

After struggling with the zipper for several minutes, the boy sighed and said, "Why does it have to be a secret?"

> Adults are always asking children what they want to be when they grow up because they're looking for ideas.
>
> PAULA POUNDSTONE

A concerned police officer approaches a boy who is crying in front of a newsstand. "What's wrong?" the cop asks.

"Superman isn't out yet!" says the boy.

"I'll handle it," the cop assures him. "Hey, Superman!" he shouts. "Come on out! We won't hurt you!"

● SOURCE: FUNNY IN CROATIA SURVEY

My five-year-old grandson was looking through some old photos when he noticed his grandfather in his Marine dress blues.

"What kind of costume is that?" he asked.

"That's not a costume," his grandfather growled. "Men have died for that uniform."

The boy looked up and said, "So you stole it, then?"

● ARLETTA LEHR

Our family was dazzled by the sights and the bustling crowds during a visit to Manhattan. "This is the city that never sleeps," I told my eleven-year-old daughter.

"That's probably because there's a Starbucks on every corner," she observed.

● LINDA FOLEY

Now that I'm a parent, I understand why my father was in a bad mood a lot.

● **ADAM SANDLER**

My cousin always "borrows" money from her older brother's piggy bank, which drives him crazy. One day, she found the piggy in, of all places, the freezer. Inside was this note: "Dear sister, I hope you'll understand, but my capital has been frozen."

● **SOURCE: FUNNY IN CHINA SURVEY**

My daughter loved the picture frame her five-year-old son bought her for Mother's Day. She found a photograph of him and replaced the cat photo that came with it. Landon became upset: "Why are you putting a picture of me in there when I bought you a picture of a cat?"

● **LORI FEENEY**

When my ex-Marine father-in-law was at my house, our six-year-old neighbor came by to play with my kids.

I asked her if she knew who he was. She looked up at him with her big blue eyes and said, "I don't remember what his name is, but I know he used to be a submarine."

● **JANELLE RAGLAND**

My cousin, a teacher, asked her young students, "Why should you never accept candy from strangers?"

One girl knew. "Because it might be past the sell-by date."

● **CHARLOTTE PRIMROSE**

A neighbor finds a young boy sitting on the stairs crying. "What's the matter, honey?" she asks him.

"It's my father," the boy says, sobbing. "He hit his finger with a hammer."

"Then why are you crying?" she says. "Because first I laughed!" he answers.

● SOURCE: FUNNY IN SERBIA SURVEY

Our friends Dave and Kristen have a precocious three-year-old. One day, Kristen chided Alayna for calling her by her first name.

"Stop calling me Kristen," she said. "I want you to call me Mommy, not Kristen."

Alayna looked confused. "But Dave calls you Kristen."

● BELVA MEEKER

YOUTH IS WASTED
ON THE YOUNG

Like all growing boys, my teenage grandson, Jermon, was constantly hungry. I went to my refrigerator to find something he might like to eat. After poking around a bit and moving the milk and juice cartons, I spotted a bowl of leftover chili.

"Hey, Jermon," I called out excitedly. He came running into the kitchen. "Look! I found some chili."

Struggling to be polite, he said, "If you're that surprised, I'm not really sure I want it."

● MARILOU FLORES

When my neighbor's granddaughter introduced me to her young son, Brian, I said to him, "My grandchildren call me Mimi. Why don't you call me that too?"

"I don't think so," he retorted, and ran off after his mother.

Later I was asked to babysit for Brian, and we hit it off wonderfully. As he snuggled up to me, he said, "I don't care what your grandchildren say. I love you, Meanie."

● MARILYN HAYDEN

Being a teenager and getting a tattoo seem to go hand and hand these days. I wasn't surprised when one of my daughter's friends showed me a delicate little Japanese symbol on her hip. "Please don't tell my parents," she begged.

"I won't," I promised. "By the way, what does that stand for?"

"Honesty," she said.

● LINDA SINGER

As a dental hygienist, I had a family come in one day for cleanings. By the time I was ready for the father, he informed me I had a lot to live up to. His six-year-old daughter kept commenting that a "very smart lady" was cleaning their teeth today.

The father said she kept going on about my intelligence until he finally had to ask what she was basing her opinion on.

The little girl replied, "I heard people in here call her the Dental High Genius."

● BARBARA GIVENS

"Donny and I are taking a year off to volunteer for the Pizza Corps."

I overheard my nine-year-old son on the phone with a friend discussing a computer simulation game. The game involved creating a family, a house for them to live in, and so on. My son, an old hand at the game, gave this warning: "Whatever you do, don't get kids. They don't bring in any money, and all they do is eat."

● NICOLE KAULING

My older son loves school, but his younger brother absolutely hates it. One weekend he cried and fretted and tried every excuse not to go back on Monday. Sunday morning on the way home from church, the crying and whining built to a crescendo. At the end of my rope, I finally stopped the car and explained, "Honey, it's a law. If you don't go to school, they'll put Mommy in jail."

He looked at me, thought a moment, then asked, "How long would you have to stay?"

● TRINA REES

Nothing seems to dim my thirteen-year-old son's sense of humor. And he's certainly not above being the butt of his own joke. Shortly after he was diagnosed with attention deficit disorder (ADD), he threw this at me: "Hey Dad—how many ADD children does it take to change a light bulb?"

"I give up," I said.

"Let's go ride our bikes."

● RICHARD HURD

The orthodontist and his assistants were removing my ten-year-old son's dental appliance. Because it was cemented to his upper teeth, they had to use some pressure to release it. When it finally popped out, three of his baby teeth came out as well.

My boy was horrified when he saw the gaps. "Well," he said to the staff gathered around him, "Who do I see about getting dentures?"

● KIM JAWORSKI

My friend Esther told me about her son's fifth-grade career day, where the children were asked, "Who knows what a psychiatrist does?"

Esther's son replied, "That's someone who asks you to lie down on a couch and then blames everything on your mother."

● CARLA GATES

I was not thrilled with the idea of letting my clueless thirteen-year-old son babysit his younger sisters, even though he begged me to.

"What about a fire?" I asked, referring to my No. 1 concern.

"Mom," he said, rolling his eyes, "I'm a Boy Scout. I know how to start a fire."

● JO WALKER

My nine-year-old and I passed a store with a sign that read "Watch Batteries Installed—$5."

He seemed confused: "Who would pay to watch batteries installed?"

● DEB MORRIS

As a dentist, I recently tried out a new chocolate-flavored pumice paste on my patients. No one liked it except for a six-year-old boy. While I polished his teeth, he continued to smile and lick his lips. "You must really like this new flavor," I said.

"Yep," he replied, nodding with satisfaction. "It tastes just like the time I dropped my candy bar in the sandbox."

● JEFFERY K. LEIBFORTH, DDS

IT'S A **KID'S WORLD**

"Kids say the darndest things."

My two sons and I were on our first white-water rafting trip. Just before a particularly nasty-looking stretch, the guide asked if anyone would like to swim the rapids. I was relieved when my seven-year-old passed, but dismayed to see my nine-year-old raise his hand. I opted, naturally, to go with him, and, safely outfitted in life jackets and helmets, we overcame our fears and swam that stretch of the river.

Later, as we changed into dry clothes back at camp, I felt such pride at what my son had accomplished that I put my arm around him and said, "You know, son, if you can swim the rapids, you can do anything in life."

"Cool!" he exclaimed. "Can I drive home?"

● TOM GILLESPIE

The night before I was to have major surgery, our nine-year-old son became worried.

"I'm scared, Mom. What if the doctor makes a mistake?"

I calmly explained that the doctor had years of experience and mistakes were unlikely.

"But what if he does?" Jeremy persisted.

"Then he'd be in a lot of trouble," I gently teased.

"You mean we could sue him," Jeremy brightened, "and I could get a new bike?"

● ARLENE M. RAUTIAINEN

My grandson, Carsen, was born with strabismus, an eye disorder. At the age of two and a half, he could speak but he was still too young to identify letters. The eye doctor therefore presented him with an eye chart made up of familiar objects such as a ball, a cat, and so on.

When the optometrist pointed to a simple drawing of an automobile, Carsen turned red with embarrassment and said he didn't know what it was. This was surprising because Carsen was a car fanatic and took pride in knowing the makes and models. He also had a large collection of matchbox toy cars.

The perplexed doctor knew the boy could see the image because he had already identified much smaller objects on the chart. "I'm sure you know what this is," he said.

With a soft stammer, Carsen answered, "Porsche?"

● GERALD JAKOVAC

Just go up to somebody on the street and say "You're it!" and then run away.

● ELLEN DEGENERES

> When I was a little kid we had a sand box. It was a quicksand box. I was an only child . . . eventually.
>
> STEVEN WRIGHT

When my daughter was seven months pregnant with a baby girl, she took my four-year-old grandson Filipe with her for an ultrasound. She explained that he was going to see his baby sister in mommy's belly. At the doctor's office, Filipe looked on radiantly while the ultrasound was made. When they arrived home, his mother, tired, sat on the sofa.

Filipe said: "I want to speak to my baby sister."

"Speak then," his mother replied.

"Okay," he said. "Open wide." He then called into his mother's gaping mouth: "Hello, sis!"

● HENRIQUE QUINTAS

We recently had to take our five-year-old son to the emergency room for an injury to his wrist from playing rugby. While we were waiting to see the doctor, a nurse came and asked if he had any allergies. I replied that he didn't have any.

"But Mom!" my son piped up. "I'm allergic to salad!"

● REBECCA KIRK

When his two front teeth fell out within days of each other, my six-year-old son, Joey, was delighted by a quick and profitable succession of visits from the Tooth Fairy. However, the novelty of having a wide gap in his smile quickly paled. Not long after, while my husband was tucking him into bed, he found two coins under Joey's pillow. When he asked what the coins were for, Joey replied firmly, "I want my teeth back."

● KAREN RITCHIE

We took our children to a restaurant named The Captain's Table. Our eldest wanted to go to the bathroom, but soon returned confused and embarrassed.

"Couldn't you find the way?" I asked him.

"Yes, I could," he replied on the verge of tears, "but I don't know if I'm a buccaneer or a wench."

● TRACY FRY

Friends of ours were just finishing their dinner one late-spring evening when suddenly they heard the chimes of the first ice cream truck of the season. Their nine-year-old son jumped up from the table and raced to the front door, hollering to his sister: "I'll go stop the truck. You stay here and beg."

● IRENE SWANTON

When my youngest son started school, I brought him to the optometrist. He was very quiet on the way over, so I asked if anything was worrying him. He stoically replied, "I was just wondering if it hurts when they take your eyes out to examine them."

● LOUISE FRAPPIER

I had the worst birthday party ever when I was a child because my parents hired a pony to give rides. And these ponies are never in good health. But this one dropped dead. It just wasn't much fun after that. One kid would sit on him and the rest of us would drag him around.

● RITA RUDNER

We recently brought our four-year-old daughter along to a doctor's appointment for my wife, who is expecting. The doctor placed a monitor on my wife's stomach, and we could hear the sound of a heartbeat.

"That's your little brother," I told our daughter.

"I know!" she replied. "Those are his footsteps."

● TOM ALBIG

SCHOOL
DAYS

" I was reading the dictionary.
I thought it was a poem about
EVERYTHING. **"**

STEVEN WRIGHT

AN APPLE FOR THE **TEACHER**

Parents are justifiably upset when their children don't get into the college of their choice. As an admissions counselor for a state university, I took a call from an irate mother demanding to know why her daughter had been turned down. Avoiding any mention of the transcript full of Ds, I explained that her daughter just wasn't as "competitive" as the admitted class. "Why doesn't she try another school for a year and then transfer?" I suggested.

"Another school!" exclaimed Mom. "Have you seen her grades?"

● SHALONDA DEGRAFFINRIED

I'd contacted a butcher to get sheep brains for a lecture in my neuroanatomy class and said I'd be by to pick them up. But when I arrived at his shop, it was closed. Taped to the door was this note: "Teacher, your brains are next door at the barbershop."

● JOHN FISHER

A middle school in New Ipswich, New Hampshire, encourages free thinking. A sign outside the school reads, "You are unique—just like everyone else."

● NAN FRONAL

Question on second-grade math quiz: "Tony drank 1/6 of a glass of juice. Emily drank 1/4 of a glass of juice. Emily drank more. Explain."

My grandson's answer: "She was more thirsty."

● JOANN MILLINGTON

"Give me a sentence about a public servant," the teacher instructed her second-grade student.

"The fireman came down the ladder pregnant," he answered.

"Um . . . do you know what pregnant means?"

"Yes," said the boy. "It means carrying a child."

● EARL B. CHILD

A schoolteacher was arrested at the airport for trying to go through security with a slide rule and a calculator. He was charged with carrying weapons of math instruction.

"I did most of it myself, but I DID get help from an 'UNNAMED SOURCE.'"

As a fundraiser, the chemistry club designed and sold T-shirts. Written across the front were our top "Stupid Chemistry Sayings":

- Have yourself a Merry Little Bismuth
- What do you do with dead people? Barium
- You stupid boron!
- We hope your year is very phosphorous.

● SHANE HART

In honor of Memorial Day, the teacher I worked with read the Constitution to her third-grade class. After reading "We the people," she paused to ask the children what they thought that meant. One boy raised his hand and asked, "Is that like 'We da bomb?'"

● RONDA DECKARD

The morning he began kindergarten, I told my son about the great adventure that awaited him. "You're going to learn so many things," I said, "like how to read and write!"

When I picked him up from school later, I asked how it went.

"Well," he said, "I still can't read or write."

● DEBBIE CRISS

Teacher: What is an evangelist?
Student: Someone who plays the evangelo.

● DONNA SAPERSTONE

I think the Discovery Channel should be on a different channel every day.

Walking through the hallways at the middle school where I work, I saw a new substitute teacher standing outside his classroom with his forehead against a locker. I heard him mutter, "How did you get yourself into this?"

Knowing he was assigned to a difficult class, I tried to offer moral support. "Are you okay?" I asked. "Can I help?"

He lifted his head and replied, "I'll be fine as soon as I get this kid out of his locker."

● HELEN BUTTON

A mind is like a parachute. It doesn't work if it is not opened.

FRANK ZAPPA

Teacher: Why can't freshwater fish live in salt water?
Student: The salt would give them high blood pressure.

● JILL SAINTE

At the school where my mother worked, the two first-grade teachers were named Miss Paine and Mrs. Hacking. One morning the mother of a student called in the middle of a flu epidemic to excuse her daughter from school.

"Is she in Paine or Hacking?" the school secretary asked.

"She feels fine," said the confused mom. "We have company and I'm just keeping her home."

● MERRI LEE COLVIN

Seen outside a professor's door at Georgetown College: "Psychology 376: Dying, Grieving, and Coping. Take for your major or minor, or as a fun elective."

● REBECCA ABBOTT

"I think someone who handles the pressures of kindergarten should be able to stay up past eight o'clock."

During my first meeting with my physically challenged students, I assured them that most people are handicapped in some way.

"Look at me," I said. "My eyes are so bad, I need to wear glasses. Because I can barely hear, I need a hearing aid. And look at my ears—they're much bigger than they should be."

From the back, a boy added, "And your nose too."

● ROBERT MEHL, SR.

STRAIGHT-A STUDENT

Driving my car one afternoon, I rolled through a stop sign. I was pulled over by a police officer, who recognized me as his former English teacher.

"Mrs. Brown," he said, "those stop signs are periods, not commas."

● GAIL BROWN

When my summer teaching post in the Czech Republic came to an end, I told my students my next teaching destination would be in Australia, "the land down under." On my final day, they presented me with a card. The carefully worded note read, "Good luck, and happy journey to the underworld."

● LOURDES H. GENOSA

A police car with flashing lights pulled me over near the high school where I teach. As the officer asked for my license and registration, my students began to drive past. Some honked their horns, others hooted, and still others stopped to admonish me for speeding.

Finally the officer asked me if I was a teacher at the school, and I told him I was.

"I think you've paid your debt to society," he concluded with a smile, and left without giving me a ticket.

● MARK JORDAN

Teacher: Mira went to the library at 5:15 and left at 6:45. How long was Mira at the library?
Student: Not long.

● LISA KARNES

A student in my math course at Ohlone State College in Fremont, Calif., developed a severe case of tendinitis. Since she couldn't write, she brought a video camera to tape my lectures. After three or four classes, I asked her if she found the method satisfactory. She said it was working quite well, even better than note-taking.

"Actually," she confessed, "I have another reason for doing this. When I told my mother you were a widower, she wanted to see what you look like."

● GERSON WHEELER

Early one morning, a mother went in to wake up her son. "Wake up, son. It's time to go to school!"

"But why, Mom? I don't want to go."

"Give me two reasons why you don't want to go."

"Well, the kids hate me for one, and the teachers hate me, too!"

"Oh, that's no reason not to go to school. Come on now and get ready."

"Give me two reasons why I should go to school."

"Well, for one, you're 52 years old. And for another, you're the principal!"

A month after Donald MacDonald started at Harvard, his mother called from Scotland. "And how are the American students, Donald?" she asked.

"They're so noisy," he complained. "One neighbor endlessly bangs his head against the wall, while another screams all night."

"How do you put up with it?"

"I just ignore them and play my bagpipes."

● MARILYN ADKINS

"Guess what?" yelled my high schooler as he burst through the door. "I got a 100 on the Spanish quiz that I didn't even know we were having."

"That's great!" I said. "But why didn't you know about the quiz?"

"Because our teacher told us about it in Spanish."

● KATHLEEN ZELL

My son, a high school senior, went to take a national literacy test recently. A sign on the classroom door read, "Literacy Testing in Progress: Do Not Distrub!"

● CATHY DILLARD

After a day of listening to my eighth graders exchange gossip, I decided to quote Mark Twain to them: "It is better to keep your mouth closed and let people think you are a fool than to open it and remove all doubt."

After considering my words, one of my students asked, "What does it mean to remove all doubt?"

● SHANNON WILSON

During my eighth-grade sex education class, no one could answer the question "What happens to a young woman during puberty?" So I rephrased it: "What happens to young women as they mature?"

One student answered: "They start to carry a purse."

● ELIZABETH ZICHA

I'm reading a great book about antigravity—I just can't put it down.

When our school librarian announced she was changing schools, my fellow teacher asked a student, "Why do you think Ms. Richardson is leaving?"

The third grader opined, "Because she's read all our books?"

● SCOTT MUIR

FAILURE IS NOT AN OPTION

I was a percussion major when I was in college, and during a rehearsal of the student orchestra, my section kept making mistakes.

"When you're too dumb to play anything," the professor conducting us sneered, "they give you a couple of sticks, put you in the back and call you a percussionist."

A friend next to me whispered, "And if you're too dumb to hang on to both sticks, they put you in the front and call you a conductor."

● JIM LOPARDO

After his first day back at school in the fall, I asked my son if the high school students were wearing anything new. "Well," he replied, "a lot of the fellows are showing up in see-through mustaches."

● BEATRICE W. COLVIN

I recently ran into an old student of mine, who said, "I always liked you. You never had favorites. You were mean to everyone."

● LOIS HENRY

When I became a licensed chiropractor, I moved back to my hometown and soon had a thriving practice. One morning I saw a new patient whom I recognized as my old high school principal.

"Gee," I said nervously, "I'm a little surprised to see you here."

"Why?" he replied. "You certainly spent a great deal of time in my office."

● D. C. REGITZ

I remember once at school we had a spelling bee, and also an ant who could tap dance.

● GARY DELANEY

Thomas Bros.

"Going to school is like playing video games . . . you've got to get through twelve levels before you're finished."

One afternoon while I was visiting my library, I noticed a group of preschoolers gathered for story time. The book they were reading was "There Was an Old Lady Who Swallowed a Fly." After the librarian finished the first page, she asked the children, "Do you think she'll die?"

"Nope," a little girl in the back said. "I saw this last night on 'Fear Factor.'"

● BRIANNE BURCL

During our computer class, the teacher chastised one boy for talking to the girl sitting next to him.

"I was just asking her a question," the boy said.

"If you have a question, ask me," the teacher tersely replied.

"Okay," he answered. "Do you want to go out with me Friday night?"

● TRACY MAXWELL

Our local newspaper lists recipients of school awards. Beneath one photo, the caption read, "This year's Perfect Attendance Awards go to Ann Stein and Bradley Jenkins. Not present for photo: Bradley Jenkins."

● ASHLEY DEROCHER

A friend was assigned a new post teaching English to inmates in prison. Feeling a little nervous on his first day, he began by asking the class a basic question:

"Now, who can tell me what a sentence is?"

● PETER MCDONAGH

My parents sent me to military school in Switzerland. There they taught me how to be neutral.

Danny was hard to miss at our school. A Civil War buff who forever wore his Confederate overcoat, he was a friend to all. When he was passed over during the vote for senior superlatives, many of us were disappointed; surely there must have been some category suitable for him.

The whole school was pleased, therefore, when the yearbook adviser surprised us with an additional photo. There was Danny, decked out in his gray coat, with the caption: "Most Likely to Secede."

● MICHAEL G. STEWART

> When they said to you at graduation "follow your dreams," did anybody say you had to wake up first?
>
> BILL COSBY

Kids have a greater need for speed than classroom computers can deliver. Impatient to turn in his term paper, one restless student kept clicking the "Print" command. The printer started to churn out copy after copy of the kid's ten-page report.

The topic? "Save Our Trees."

● KEN CUMMINGS

During a grammar lesson Mrs O'Neill said, "Paul, give me a sentence with a direct object."

Paul replied, "Everyone thinks you are the best teacher in the school."

"Thank you, Paul," said Mrs O'Neill, "but what is the object?"

"To get the best mark possible," said Paul.

● SHAUN MILLER

Teacher: Millie, give me a sentence starting with i.
Millie: I is . . .
Teacher: No, Millie. Always say, "I am."
Millie: Okay, I am the ninth letter of the alphabet.

One of our projects at military leadership school called for us to speak in front of the class on a topic picked by our instructor. A classmate gave an impassioned speech on the benefits of drinking liquor. Alcohol, he insisted, warded off colds, kept you alert, and even made you steadier on your feet.

"Good job," said our instructor when he finished. "Only one thing: Your topic was the benefits of drinking liquids, not liquor."

● DAVID WILSON

At the beginning of my junior year at Russellville High School in Arkansas, our homeroom teacher had us fill out a form stating our future goals. Out of curiosity, I leaned over to see what my friend put down for her aspirations.

Where it read "Vocational Plans," she had written, "Florida."

● CRYSTAL BRUCE

When my sister was in high school, she went out with the captain of the chess team. My parents loved him 'cause they figured any guy who took three hours to make a move was okay.

● COMIC BRIAN KILEY

An e-mail from our school principal: "The Miss BHS Beauty Pageant has been moved to Friday night instead of Saturday because of the contestants involved in the hog show."

● VASTER FRYAR

"Hurry up or we'll be late!" shouts a teacher to her kindergarten class.

"What's the rush?" a tot asks coolly.

"If we're late, we'll miss your next class!" the teacher reminds him.

The kid shrugs. "If you're in such a hurry, go on without us."

● SOURCE: FUNNY IN THAILAND SURVEY

Father: The fortune teller said my son would excel in school.

Friend: And did he?

Father: Yes. The size of his uniform is XL.

● RAJESHWARI SINGH

TEACHER'S PET

On the first day of Hebrew School the teacher finished the lessons and asked for questions.

"I've got one," said a boy. "According to the Bible, the Children of Israel crossed the Red Sea, right?"

"That's right," said the teacher.

"And the Children of Israel defeated the Philistines and the Egyptians and they built the temple, and they were always doing something important, right?"

"All of that is correct," agreed the instructor. "So what's the question?"

"Well," demanded the boy. "What were the grownups doing?"

● CLARENCE KRAJENKE

"I did my homework but the dog pressed control-alt-delete."

The new family in the neighborhood overslept and their six-year-old daughter missed her school bus. Though late for work, her father had to drive her to classes, following her directions.

The trip took 20 minutes around a number of turns, yet the school proved to be just a short distance from their home. Annoyed, the father asked his daughter why she had given such directions.

"That's the only way I know, Daddy," she explained. "That's where the school bus goes."

● JOHN MCGEORGE

I went to a really tough high school. In English class my teacher told us to make an outline, and someone asked, "Where's the body?"

● JAY TRACHMAN

A boy comes home from school and asks his mother, "Ma, what's sex?"

Frazzled, the mother stops what she's doing and starts to explain, beginning with the little seed, talking about the birds and the bees and finally about man.

Slightly taken aback, the boy observes the extremely thorough lesson. There's something solemn to the moment.

Once she is through, the mother asks, "Did you understand, honey?"

The answer came in a flash, "Yes, Mom. Except that all the stuff you told me is not going to fit in this little square . . ."

Only then did she notice that he held a form to be filled out with his name, age, sex . . .

Where there was a little space to fill in M or F.

● MÁRCIA SOUZA

"Mom, I won't go to school anymore."
"Why, my dear?"

"It doesn't make sense. I can't read yet, and they don't let me talk."

● ANDRÁSNÉ PLÓSZ

I don't know how to speed-read. Instead, I listen to Books on Tape on fast-forward.

Sylvia: "Dad, can you write in the dark?"
Father: "I think so. What do you want me to write?"
Sylvia: "Your signature on this school report card."

● ANDREA MARRIAGE

A high school student is taking an oral exam on Contemporary History. Since he obviously doesn't know much, he's nervous, stutters and gives incomplete answers—a real disaster. The teacher, a good person at heart, intent on helping the student, says:

"Don't be nervous, relax. I'm going to ask you one last question, and if you answer correctly you'll pass."

"Thank you teacher."

"So here it goes, what was Hitler's first name?"

The student smiles, breathes in confidently and replies: "Heil. Heil Hitler!"

● JOÃO MENDONÇA FERREIRA

Headmistress: I hear you missed school yesterday.
Pupil: No Ma'am, not a bit.

● MICHAEL MATHEW

My eight-year-old brother was doing his homework but was stumped by a math question. "Katie," he asked our six-year-old sister, "what would I get if I added seven apples and six apples?"

"I don't know," she replied. "In my math class, we use oranges."

● STEWART SUTHERLAND

Never trust a man with a tassel on his loafer.
It's like, What, did your foot just graduate?

It was the first day of kindergarten for my oldest daughter, so I took her to wait for the school bus with my son, age three and a half. I didn't really want it to show, but I was feeling sad, and as soon as she was gone I began to cry. My son did the same.

The next day, we took her to the bus stop again. This time, I held back my tears when the bus had left, and Louis-Pierre immediately inquired: "Are we crying today, Mommy?"

● MANON BRÛLÉ

> My dog licked the crumbs out of my computer keyboard and earned an online college degree.
>
> @SCBCHBUM

Did you hear about the cannibal who was expelled from school?

He was buttering up his teacher.

A secondary-school student came home one night rather depressed. "What's the matter, son?" asked his father.

"Bad news, Dad," said the boy. "It's my grades. They're all wet."

"What do you mean 'all wet'?"

"Below C-level," replied the son.

● JEANNIE SANUSI

At the beginning of the school year, I mentioned to a first-grade student that he'd grown a lot since I'd seen him the year before. "I've been doing a lot of that, growing and shrinking."

Puzzled, I asked what he meant. "Well, I used to be up to my big brother's nose," he replied, "but now I'm only up to his chin."

● BARB SODERQUIST

"Can people predict the future?" my seven-year-old granddaughter, Cassandra, asked her older, wiser sisters.

"Yes," Rebecca replied, "Mom can."

"Really?" Samantha exclaimed.

"Yep," Rebecca continued. "She can take one look at your report card and tell you what will happen when Dad gets home."

● LOUISE KERR

"Daddy, they call me Mafioso at school."

"Don't worry, son. I'll take care of it tomorrow."

"OK Dad, but please make it look like an accident."

● TANIA CARPINELLI

"Who were the first people in the Garden of Eden?" asked the Sunday school teacher.

Replied one small child, "The Adams family."

● PAT ELPHINSTONE

First mother: "How's your son getting on at medical school?"

Second mother: "I don't know, I can't read his letters."

● FRED PEGG

TAKE ME OUT TO THE BALL GAME

" Our hometown baseball team is called the Possums. They get killed on the road. "

RICHARD KLIMKIEWICZ

SUPERSTARS

My high-school basketball team was scheduled to play in the district tournament, and when we got there we were all excited to find our pictures and our stats published in the glossy program. My friend Brian Bird, a senior who was having a great season, eagerly searched for his name. But then he threw the program down in disgust, and I figured that there must be some error in his entry.

Sure enough, his name appeared as "Bird, Brain."

● DARREN JOHNSON

In honor of our armed forces, the University of South Carolina football team used the backs of players' jerseys to display a little patriotism. They placed words like Duty, Service, Courage, and Commitment where players' names would normally go. During the game against the University of Florida, a fight broke out, prompting the television commentator to announce, "It looked like Integrity threw the first punch."

● MIKE GADELL

My husband, a big-time sports fan, was watching a football game with our grandchildren. He had just turned 75 and was feeling a little wistful. "You know," he said to our grandson, Nick, "it's not easy getting old. I guess I'm in the fourth quarter now."

"Don't worry, Grandpa," Nick said cheerily. "Maybe you'll go into overtime."

● EVELYN BREDLEAU

At five-ten and 114 pounds, our son, Dan, is the skinniest player on his high school football team. During one of his games, I remarked to a cousin, "I wonder why they gave him the uniform with the number 1 on it."

"It's probably the only one that fit," she said.

● DIANE FELDMAN

A five-year-old at my church proudly announced to me that he had scored five goals in his last soccer match and that his team had won the game.

His mother added, "It was close though. The final score was 3-2."

● JEFF KINGSWOOD

The night before she was to attend a celebrity golf tournament, my friend Irene went to a party in honor of the event. Several of the famous athletes who were playing in the tournament were at the door greeting guests. Among them was Joe Montana, the pro football Hall of Fame quarterback and Super Bowl winner. Shaking my friend's hand, he said, "Hi! Joe Montana."

She didn't know Joe Montana from Joe Six-Pack, so in all sincerity she extended her hand and said, "Irene. Minnesota."

● ROGER LEE

My nine-year-old grandson Michael wiped the sweat from his face while taking a quick break from his soccer game. The coach ordered him back on the field.

"I'm so tired," Michael moaned.

"You're too young to be that tired," the coach countered.

"Well," Michael persisted, "I'm 63 in dog years."

● COLLEEN LACHNER

Our high school has lots of spirit, but that didn't help the football team, who had yet to win a game. So when our principal saw some cheerleaders sitting in the stands, he asked, "Don't you think you girls should be down there cheering for your team?"

"I think," one of them said, "we should be down there playing for our team."

● EMILY KARNES

Just play. Have fun. Enjoy the game.

● MICHAEL JORDAN

After his football team won the Sugar Bowl, my brother received a championship ring. On it was Mike's name, his number, the team mascot and, in the center, a blue field with No. 1 spelled out in diamonds.

Although thrilled, my brother wondered if it wasn't a little ostentatious. My father assured him it was a badge of honor, a tribute to all the hard work he had done—and that he should wear it with pride. Just then my mother walked into the room. Glancing at the ring, she said, "Boy, is that thing ever gaudy."

● ROBERT STILLMAN

> Anyone who's just driven 90 yards against huge men trying to kill them has earned the right to do jazz hands.
>
> CRAIG FERGUSON

SUPERFANS

A buddy of mine, Mike, had season tickets to the Detroit Lions football games. Last year they had such a miserable record that he couldn't give away two tickets to a game he wasn't able to attend. While parking at a mall, he decided to leave the tickets under his windshield wiper. "And that worked?" I asked.

"Not exactly," said Mike. "I returned to find six more tickets to the same game."

● JOSEPH L. FROMM

Lying battered and bruised in hospital, a man explained to his friend, "I told my wife that when the football is on TV, it would take a team of wild horses to drag me away. I still have no idea where she got them."

● JEFFREY CRUNKHORN

"Actually, I'd much rather take guitar lessons,
but he so looks forward to hockey season."

About to have a blood test, I nervously waited while the nurse tightened a tourniquet around my arm. "I understand you're from Oklahoma," she said. "Are you a Sooners fan?"

"Absolutely!" I replied.

"Well," she continued as she raised the needle, "this may hurt a little. I'm from Nebraska."

● JANET THOMPSON

On a Saturday afternoon when football fever was running high in South Bend, Indiana, a Notre Dame student was brought into the hospital where I was on duty as a nurse. He had acute appendicitis, and as I prepared him for surgery I asked if he wasn't terribly disappointed to miss the big game.

"Oh, I won't miss it," he said. "Doc is giving me a spinal anesthetic so I can listen to it during the operation!"

● RITA HAMILTON

After a high school basketball game, the coach spotted a cell phone lying on the floor. "Here," he said to the ref, "I think this is yours."

"What makes you think it's my phone?" asked the ref.

"Easy," the coach said. "It says you have ten missed calls."

● JANET KEENEY

I was glued to the TV. It looked like the pitcher would throw a no-hitter. My wife, who thinks baseball is boring, wondered why the crowd was so excited.

"It's a perfect game," I told her. "Do you know what that is?"

"Yeah," she said, "one that's over."

● BOB RAPP

While I was working security at a football game, a fan spilled beer on a cheerleader's pom-poms. As a favor, I rinsed them off in the men's room. As I shook off the water, someone came out of a stall. Stunned, he announced, "That's the first time anyone's cheered me on while going to the bathroom."

● RUBEN CHAVEZ

> Whoever said "It's not whether you win or lose that counts" probably lost.
>
> MARTINA NAVRATILOVA

Football finally makes sense. A guy took his blonde girlfriend to her first football game. They had great seats right behind their team's bench. After the game, he asked her how she liked the experience.

"Oh, I really liked it," she replied, "especially the tight pants and all the big muscles, but I just couldn't understand why they were killing each other over 25 cents."

Dumbfounded, her date asked, "What do you mean?"

"Well, they flipped a coin. One team got it, and then for the rest of the game, all they kept screaming was, 'Get the quarter back! Get the quarter back!' I'm like, Hello-o-o? It's only 25 cents!"

● MELISSA JONES

GET YOUR **GAME FACE ON**

I had the pleasure of watching my ten-year-old nephew's final soccer game of the season. They were not doing well—they were losing 10-0 with two minutes left. But then they got a break and scored.

The team went crazy! The parents went crazy! The coaches went crazy! Everybody was jumping up and down as if they had won the championship.

When the kids came off the field, I caught up to my nephew as the celebrations continued. Puzzled, I asked, "What's going on?"

"You don't understand," he said. "That's the only goal we scored all year!"

● SHARON MAJOR

My eight-year-old grandson, Cylus, has been losing his baby teeth over the last few months. Showing the loss of another tooth at the dinner table, he turned to his mom with his big grin and said: "Look, I am a hockey player!"

● PENNY KELLETT

A university rugby coach called out to the new team member, saying: "Look, I'm not supposed to have you on this team because you failed your math exams. But we really need you, so I'll ask you one simple math question and if you answer it correctly, I'll sign a slip to say you've passed math, OK?" The player nodded.

"Right," said the coach. "What's seven times six?"

The player wrinkled his forehead and thought for a while, then replied, "Forty-two!"

Immediately all the other team members shouted, "Aw, come on, coach. Give him another chance!"

● FELICITY ROONEY

My parents attended our son Ryan's soccer game one night. After the game, my dad was tickling Ryan when the lad looked up and warned him, "Don't forget, Grandpa, Mom says if you wind me up, you have to take me home."

● DEBORAH HUBER

If a woman has to choose between catching a fly ball and saving an infant's life, she will choose to save the infant's life without even considering if there are men on base.

● DAVE BARRY

My son had gone to see a soccer match earlier in the day, and I made a special effort to avoid hearing the score so I could enjoy the match on TV later.

As I settled down to watch it, my son joined me so he could see the goals again. One team scored early on in the game. "Right then," said my son immediately afterwards. "I'm off to bed."

● D. JOLLY

Hate to say it, but our high school football team isn't very good. One day the coach spotted the marching band practicing on the field and told them to get off before they tore it up.

"Can we march in the end zone?" asked a band member. "The team never uses that."

● D.A.

Our seventeen-year-old daughter was going by bus to a soccer tournament in Delaware and she'd packed more baggage than Noah. As I was hauling it out of the trunk, I sarcastically remarked, "Oh, Erica, we forgot the kitchen sink!"

Another father chimed in: "It's okay. Ashley has one—they can share."

● ANDREW W. DENCS

My thirteen-year-old son, Waylon, had been playing a lot of hockey games, and one Sunday we attended church before his next game. We knew Waylon had been on the rink too much when, at the end of the service, as we lined up to greet the pastor, he shook the pastor's hand and said, "Good game."

● LORILL DURANT

"When I was young my father and I played catch."

After not firing a gun for years, I visited a nearby pistol range. I was awful—couldn't hit a thing. Turning to my friend, who was watching, I said, "I know it may be hard to believe, but I was on my school's shooting team."

He asked, "What were you—the target?"

● FRANK DAVIS

My five-year-old nephew, Eric, went with his dad to see his first hockey game.

Arriving home, he told his mom about the fight two players got into, and she asked why the men were fighting.

Eric responded: "They fight because they don't know how to play hockey!"

● LISA KINGHAM

We brought our hockey-crazy eighteen-month-old grandson to church at Easter. During the children's focus, Joshua stayed with us and stood on the pew to see what was going on up front. The minister talked about Christ rising from the dead. He asked the children to raise their arms and shout, "Hallelujah!" each time he said, "Christ is risen!"

Joshua watched with interest the first time they went through this exercise. However, the second time the minister said, "Christ is risen!" Joshua, standing on the pew with arms raised high, yelled, "SCORES!"

● JANE MCDONALD

I thought my eight-year-old grandson was perhaps growing out of his timid stage when he arrived home from a hockey game announcing, "I got a penalty, Grandpa."

"What for?" I asked.

"Too many men on the ice," he replied.

● ROBERT HORAN

My six-year-old son, Austin, recently became interested in hockey cards, so I bought him a collector's booklet and a starter set. While completing a page, he paused to ask me, "Dad, what were the New Jersey Devils called before they got their new jerseys?"

● LEE GILES

The rules of football and the plot of *The Godfather* are the two most complicated things that every guy understands no matter how dumb he is.

● JULIAN MCCULLOUGH

After collecting bugs with her two brothers all summer, I thought it would be a nice change for my six-year-old daughter to see a hockey game. Shortly after the game began, she asked what a penalty was.

I told her a player was sent to the penalty box if he tripped another player. Caring for all those bugs must have still been on her mind because she then asked, "Daddy, do they cut holes in the lid of the box so the player can breathe?"

● DANIEL RODRIGUE

> Golf is a game in which you yell "fore," shoot six, and write down five.
>
> PAUL HARVEY

One day at the bank where I worked as a teller, an elderly gentleman presented me with a check; unfortunately, he had no ID. Keenly aware of the growing line behind him, he dug through his pockets to no avail. Suddenly his face lit up. He grinned and pointed to his head.

"There's my name on my cap!"

Sure enough, the name on his hat was the same as the one on the cheque. Then he leaned forward and whispered conspiratorially, "Actually, it's my son's cap, but we've got the same name."

● GRACE DIFALCO

After years of watching his older brother, it was finally Jesse's turn to play on a hockey team. We encouraged him at home, and I attended every one of his practices.

We thought he was enjoying himself until one day before practice he turned to me and sighed, "If you like hockey so much, Mom, why don't you play?"

● JANET GASTALDO

They say that nobody is perfect. Then they tell you practice makes perfect. I wish they'd make up their minds.

● WILT CHAMBERLAIN

Tara, my wife, hates watching sports. So it was no surprise when, at her brother's home one day watching the hockey playoffs, she moaned and groaned about how boring it all was. But when our team scored the winning goal and everyone leaped up and yelled "Yahoo!" including my wife, I was taken aback.

"What are you so excited about?" my brother-in-law asked Tara. "I thought you hated hockey."

"I do," she answered. "I'm just glad it's over!"

● DWAYNE A. ANDERSON

Not quite grasping the sanctity of "Hockey Night in Canada," I plunked myself next to my new husband one Saturday night to chat. He was distracted by the action on TV, and after being shushed a few times, I gave him a "look." Immediately contrite, he picked up the remote. "I'm sorry, honey," he apologized, "I'm being rude. You go ahead and talk—I'll just turn up the volume."

● C. EPP

One of my five-year-old son's baseball games was rained out, so at the next practice the coach explained to the kids that he was going to schedule a makeup game.

One of the players became very indignant and said that there was no way he was going to play a makeup game. In fact, he didn't even like makeup!

● JENNIFER ADAMS

ALL BETS ARE **OFF**

Tyler, my four-year-old son, went to a local baseball game with my mother-in-law. At the park, she gave him money to buy a treat from the concession booth. When he returned, she asked for the change.

Tyler patted his pocket. "This is mine," he stated.

Then, pointing to the woman in the booth, he added, "She has yours."

● KELLY CHRISTO

At my home games during softball season, Mom was always the loudest fan. My two younger brothers came along to play with the smaller children in the sandbox behind the bleachers.

In the seventh inning of one game, as our pitcher was beginning her windup for what we hoped would be the last batter, Mom spotted several of the sandbox crew with arms raised and fists full of sand. In her most motherly tone, she shouted, "Don't throw that!"

The pitcher and all the other players immediately froze.

● KIMBERLEY REED

One afternoon I was watching a football game when my wife, Sophia, asked, "Sweetheart, can you help me with the dishes?"

Lazy as I am, I called to five-year-old Jase, "Son, go help Mommy with the dishes. You'll need the skills in the future to help your wife with the chores."

"Why?" he asked, "I can just let my son do them for me!"

● JESSE YALCHIN

Puttering round his local supermarket, the chairman of the world's worst football team spotted an elderly lady struggling with her basket of shopping.

"Excuse me," he said. "Can you manage?"

"Yes," the lady replied. "But I don't want the job."

● ROY BERRY

Watching soccer on TV, my father started complaining about one of the players. "He's got two left feet," he shouted. "I don't understand why they let him play at all!"

"Maybe," said my little brother quietly, "it's his ball."

● PAUL MCAULEY

I fell while playing touch football at a company outing, breaking my arm rather badly. When my wife saw the crowd gathered around me, she came running over, took one look at my arm—and fainted.

My son then came over, looked at his mother, saw my broken arm—and promptly threw up. Then my two preteen daughters came upon us. "What's wrong with Mom?"

Not wanting to alarm them, I said: "Just the heat, girls. She'll be fine in a minute."

"What's up with Ed?"

"Just something he ate," I replied.

"And you, Dad. What's wrong?"

"A broken arm, but I'll be just fine," I assured them.

After considering the facts for a moment, they asked: "Well, could we have ten dollars? The snack bar is closing in five minutes."

● HUGH FRASER

> **My dad didn't text me after the Patriots game, which is basically a Life Alert signal if you're from New England.**
>
> @JOSHGONDELMAN

After my daughter sat glued to the TV set for most of the day, I told her, "Do you know that the average American spends more hours per day watching TV than the average Olympic athlete spends training?"

She replied, "What's the point of all that training if no one's going to watch?"

● DAVE KOLACZ

As a mother of four, I spend a lot of time providing taxi service to soccer games, football practice, and dance classes. But I didn't realize just how much time it was until someone asked my three-year-old where he lived. "In my car seat," he said.

● CONNIE REDWINE

A chicken was playing in a soccer match and scored two goals.

"You're playing very well," the referee said. "Do you train hard?"

"Yes, I do," replied the chicken. "But it's not easy. I'm a lawyer and don't have much free time."

With that the referee immediately pulled out the red card and ordered the chicken off of the pitch.

"Why did you do that?" demanded the chicken's teammates.

"Professional fowl," said the referee.

● KEN CHAPMAN

Talk about a freak accident. My uncle was driving to a hockey game with his two sons when their car hit a low-flying duck.

After absorbing the shock of what just happened, Uncle Mike broke the silence with, "There's a bird that didn't live up to his name."

● JASON BULBUK

On a brutally humid day, I walked past a miniature golf course and saw a dad following three small children from hole to hole.

"Who's winning?" I shouted.

"I am," said one kid.

"Me," said another.

"No, me," yelled the third.

Sweat dripping down his face, the dad gasped, "Their mother is."

● TOM LAPPAS

When our son was about four months old, I caught sight of my husband in another room, holding the baby on his lap, talking to him and pointing. I was touched by this father/son bonding, and went into the room to eavesdrop.

"Football," my husband said slowly, pointing to the TV. "This is football."

● JUDY WATSON

A famous soccer player calls his pregnant wife, "How's our baby?"

"I have good and bad news."

"What's the good news?"

"He's been kicking around a lot."

"And what's the bad news?"

"He hurt his knee."

● ROBERTO DA SILVA

My short-sighted son hated playing football at school. He wasn't allowed to wear his glasses and his inability to spot the ball led to many embarrassing incidents.

But none of these compared to the day he collided with someone and apologized profusely. Not seeing the ball is one thing, but saying sorry to the goalpost—how do you live that down?

● EVE YAGNIK

I think foosball is a combination of soccer and shishkabobs.

● MITCH HEDBERG

My two-year-old son, Lucas, was determined to buy a new toy at the dollar store. We were waiting in line to pay for a carefully chosen set of toy golf clubs when Lucas announced, "Mommy, we forgot to get something!"

"What's that?" I asked.

"The hole!"

● CHARLYN BARRINGTON

For the second time in a row, I was forced to impose on the woman with whom I carpooled to our children's soccer practices. I phoned and explained that my husband had the car again, so I wouldn't be able to take my turn.

A few minutes before she was due to pick up my son, my husband showed up. Since it was too late for me to call and say I could drive after all, I asked my husband to hide the car in the garage and to stay inside. I also explained to my son that he shouldn't mention anything about his father's whereabouts. Unfortunately, my husband forgot and was in front of our house chatting with a friend when my carpool partner arrived. When my son returned from practice, I asked him if she had noticed.

"Yes," he replied, "she asked me which of the two men in front of the house was my father. But don't worry. I told her I didn't know."

● CECILIA RODRIGUEZ

The crowds were gathering on Mount Olympus to watch a soccer match between the gods and mortals. As the teams ran out on to the pitch, the manager of the mortals asked the manager of the gods, "Who's that character that's half human and half horse?"

"Oh," replied the god's manager, "that's our centaur forward."

● BRIAN ELLIOT

BRAVE NEW WORLD

> ❝ USER: the word computer professionals use when they mean 'idiot.' ❞
>
> **DAVE BARRY**

TECHNOLOGY **FAIL**

Our grandson's scoutmaster must have fainted when he saw what he'd texted to his troop's parents: "Scouts 7:00 Sharp at the Church. We will finish up Aviation, Cycling, and Gynecology Merit Badges."

That was followed by this message three minutes later: "Change of Plans. We will not be finishing up the Gynecology Merit Badge. Instead, it will be the Genealogy Merit Badge."

● CAROL ALLISON

". . . and what's his domain name?"

mentioned to my sons that some teens used Facebook to plan a robbery at a local mall.

"How did the NSA miss that?" my twenty-one-year-old asked.

"I told you guys," said my seventeen-year-old. "No one uses Facebook anymore."

● MARY-HEATHER REYNOLDS

A month ago, my friend announced on Facebook that she was no longer ordering the large Coke at McDonald's and would order only the small size. But the other day, looking to satisfy a craving, she drove up to the intercom at the drive-through and ordered a large soft drink. A disembodied voice replied, "I thought you were cutting back."

● JULIE ENGELHARDT

I love the self-checkout aisle at my supermarket. The only problem comes when I leave an item on the scanner too long and the robo-voice scolds, "Please move your whole milk [or whatever] to the bagging area." Ordinarily, I just ignore it. But on my last shopping trip, I moved fast when the voice began shouting, "Please move your pork butt."

● LARRY MORETZ

Students at Iowa State University proved once and for all that the computer just can't replace human calculations. They held an "IBM mixer" dance, where each student fed his vital statistics and interests into a computer and was then paired off with a member of the opposite sex who, the computer said, was most suited to him.

Imagine the chagrin of one coed who ended up with her twin brother.

● JIM CHAMPION

> A computer once beat me at chess, but it was no match for me at kickboxing.
>
> EMO PHILIPS

GPS GONE WILD

Simon Cowell: This entire trip has been simply ghastly. You missed two turns, and your side-view mirrors weren't adjusted properly. And the worst part was the singing to the radio. Just awful. You're no longer in the driver's seat. In fact, I'd be surprised if you returned next week—because you'd probably get lost again.

Jack Bauer: I don't have a lot of time. You're going to have to trust me. The country's fate is in my hands. So please, listen to me. The Walmart is on the left, 2.6 miles up the road. Today's the last day for the rollback prices on that wicker hamper you want, so grab it and go. Then we have some business to take care of.

***The Biggest Loser* trainers:** Come on! So you're lost. Are you gonna cry? Don't you dare reach for that glove compartment. I know that's where you hide your Twix bars. Just take a breath. Pull over. Do some stretching. Get back in. And let's turn around and get back on track! There's a weigh station on the right.

● READER'S DIGEST

I was feeling pretty creaky after hearing the TV reporter say, "To contact me, go to my Facebook page, follow me on Twitter, or try me the old-fashioned way—e-mail."

● LEE EVANS

A wife texts her husband on a frosty winter's morning. "Windows frozen!"

Her husband texts back, "Pour lukewarm water over it."

Five minutes later comes her reply: "Computer completely messed up now."

● CATHERIN HISCOX

I was showing my kids an old rotary phone when my nine-year-old asked, "How did you text on it?"

My fifteen-year-old daughter roared with laughter, until a thought occurred to her: "Wait, where did you store your contacts?"

● TARA PRICE

The computer in my high school classroom was acting up. After watching me struggle with it, a student explained that my hard drive had crashed. So I called IT. "Can someone look at my computer?" I asked. "The hard drive crashed."

"We can't just send people down on your say-so," said the specialist. "How do you know that's the problem?"

"A student told me."

"We'll send someone right over."

● ROLF EKLUND

My husband, a computer-systems trouble-shooter, rode with me in my new car one afternoon. He had been working on a customer's computer all morning and was still tense from the session. When I stopped for a traffic light, I made sure to leave a safe distance from the stop line to keep oncoming drivers from hitting the car.

I couldn't help but laugh when my husband impatiently waved at me to move the car forward while saying, "Scroll up, honey."

● GEORGIA M. HARVEY

I'd like the window that says, "Are you sure you want to do this? OK/Cancel" to pop up less often on my computer and more in my real life.

● @AARONFULLERTON

My boyfriend Hans and I met online. After dating a long time, I introduced him to my uncle, who was fascinated by the fact that we met over the Internet. He asked Hans what kind of line he had used to pick me up. Ever the geek, Hans naively replied, "I just used a modem."

● ANNE MCCONNELL

It was my friend's first camping trip with her husband, and they were lost. He tried all the usual tactics to determine direction—moss on the trees (there was none), direction of the sun (it was overcast), and so on. Just as she began to panic, he spotted a cabin in the distance. "This way," he said as he led her back to their camp.

"How did you do that?" my friend asked.

"Simple. In this part of the country, the satellite dishes point south."

● MARY ALICE BEHE

WORLD WIDE **WEB**

I purchased a new desktop-publishing program that surprised me by containing a make-a-paper-airplane option. I decided to give it a try. After I selected the plane I wanted, the software gave me a choice of accessories available for my plane, including a stick-up tail, adjustable flaps and an AM/FM radio. Out of curiosity I chose the AM/FM radio.

The program responded with a message box stating: "Come on, be serious. These are just paper airplanes."

● GREG SCOTT

A solar-powered computer wristwatch, which is programmed to tell the time and date for 125 years, has a guarantee—for two years.

● EMIL L. BIRNBAUM

"I'll miss you, Great-Grandma," wrote my mother's great-grandson in an e-mail he sent before shipping out to Iraq.

"I'll miss you too, dear," she responded. "Stay safe. LOL, Great-Grandma."

Poor Mom didn't realize that LOL doesn't stand for "lots of love."

● JEANNE HENDRICKSON

"When I was your age, I could tweet without a phone."

Playing around with my new iTouch, I decided to get directions to my son's base from my home in Maryland. So I typed "Wahiawa, Hawaii." I got turn-by-turn directions until I hit the coast. Then I was told, "Kayak across the Pacific Ocean entering Hawaii."

● CINDY HAYS

I hide photos on my computer of me petting animals at the zoo in a file named Fireworks and Vacuums so my dog won't find them.

● @ELITERRY

Our newer, high-speed computer was in the shop for repair, and my son was forced to work on our old model with the black-and-white printer.

"Mom," he complained to me one day, "this is like we're living back in the twentieth century."

● DENISE PERRY DONAVIN

After we got broadband Internet, my husband decided to start paying bills online. This worked great; in fact all our bill companies accepted online payments except one—our Internet service provider.

● SARAH LIBERA

There are only two types of computers in the world: those that waste your precious time and those that waste your precious time faster.

● ANONYMOUS

earning to use a voice-recognition computer program, I was excited about the prospect of finally being able to write more accurately than I type. First I read out loud to the computer for about an hour to train it to my voice, then I opened a clean page and dictated a nursery rhyme to see the magic.

The computer recorded: "Murry fed a little clam, its fleas was bright and slow."

● CARRIE E. PITTS

realized the impact of computers on my young son one evening when there was a dramatic sunset. Pointing to the western sky, David said, "I wish we could click and save that."

● THERESA KLEIN

THE JOY OF TEXTING

NOT EVERYONE HAS MASTERED THE ART OF TEXTING. CASE IN POINT:

MOM: Stop at dollar store on way home and get lunch maggots.

ME: Lunch maggots?

MOM: Baffles.

MOM: Baggies.

MOM: Ziploc lunch Baggies.

MOM: Spell-check is not helping me.

MOM: By the way, this is Dad.

● FROM WHENPARTENTSTEXT.COM

I was preparing lunch for my granddaughter when the phone rang. "If you can answer one question," a young man said, "you'll win ten free dance lessons."

Before I could tell him I was not interested, he continued. "You'll be a lucky winner if you can tell me what Alexander Graham Bell invented."

"I don't know," I replied dryly, trying to discourage him.

"What are you holding in your hand right now?" he asked excitedly.

"A bologna sandwich."

"Congratulations!" he shrieked. "And for having such a great sense of humor . . ."

● LOLA CANTRELL

A large outdoor thermometer I had sent my son in Florida hung by his pool. One day he and his wife were standing beside it discussing the temperature. Scott was comparing the Fahrenheit scale to the Celsius scale when suddenly his eight-year-old daughter interrupted.

"Dad, is that what the F and the C on the thermometer stand for?"

Told that was right, she said, "Gee, all this time I thought they meant Florida and Canada."

● JESSIE SNOW

My fifty-something friend Nancy and I decided to introduce her mother to the magic of the Internet. Our first move was to access the popular "Ask Jeeves" site, and we told her it could answer any question she had.

Nancy's mother was very skeptical until Nancy said, "It's true, Mom. Think of something to ask it."

As I sat with fingers poised over the keyboard, Nancy's mother thought a minute, then responded, "How is Aunt Helen feeling?"

● CATHERINE BURNES

On one occasion while my niece Lupita was in preschool, in our eagerness to help her remember what it was she had learned during the week, my sister wrote the symbol "+" on a piece of paper and asked the girl: "What sign is this?"

"It's a plus," she responded.

"And what is it used for?" we asked.

With an air of independence, she answered: "Well, it's for turning up the volume on the television!"

● MARTHA CUATECONTZI XOCHITIOTZI

A father shows up at his daughter's home and finds his son-in-law angrily packing his bags.

"What's wrong?" he asks.

"I texted my wife that I was coming home today from my golfing trip. And what did I find when I walked through the door? Her making out with Joe Murphy! I'm leaving!"

"Now, calm down," says his father-in-law. "There must be a simple explanation. I'll find out what happened." Moments later, he reappears. "I told you there was a simple explanation, and there is," he says. "She never got your text."

I realized my little nephew will never know life without Facebook. He'll never know what it's like to go, "I wonder what happened to that guy Chris from high school?" and then just shrug his shoulders and move on.

● COMEDIAN OPHIRA EISENBERG

The Internet also makes it extraordinarily difficult for me to focus. One small break to look up exactly how almond milk is made, and four hours later I'm reading about the Donner Party and texting all my friends: "Did you guys know about the Donner Party and how messed up that was?"

● MINDY KALING

As my sister relaxed on the couch, her head comfortably leaning against the crook of her husband's arm, her cell phone beeped. It was a text message from her husband: "Move."

● AMBER CARIKER

As an assistant high-school track coach, I recorded the results of each home meet and made copies for all the coaches. But because our track shed did not have electricity, I had to use carbon paper. A freshman team member offered to help, and I showed her how to place the carbon paper shiny side down so that the image would transfer to the sheet beneath it.

"What will they think of next?" she said in astonishment. "Pretty soon we won't need copy machines anymore."

● BARBARA LOOMIS

NO THOUGHT IS TOO RANDOM, NO GRIEVANCE TOO PETTY, TO KEEP US FROM ORGANIZING A GROUP. OUR FAVORITES:

1. Students Against Backpacks with Wheels

2. When I Was Your Age Pluto Was a Planet

3. People Who Always Have to Spell Their Names for Other People

4. No, I Don't Care if I Die at 12 a.m., I Refuse to Pass On Your Chain Letter

5. Friends Don't Let Friends Wear Crocs

6. I Secretly Want to Punch Slow-Walking People in the Back of the Head

7. I Don't Care if the Spider Is Not Hurting Anyone, I Want It Dead!

8. I Am Fluent in Three Languages: English, Sarcasm, and Profanity

9. I Will Carry 20 Grocery Bags So I Don't Have to Make a Second Trip

10. An Arbitrary Number of People Demanding That Some Sort of Action Be Taken

A helicopter was flying toward Seattle when an electrical malfunction disabled all of the aircraft's navigation and communications equipment. Due to the extreme haze that day, the pilot now had no way of determining the course to the airport. All he could make out was a tall building nearby, so he moved closer to it, quickly wrote out a large sign reading, "Where am I?" and held it in the chopper's window.

Responding quickly, the people in the building penned a large sign of their own. It read: "You are in a helicopter."

The pilot smiled, and within minutes he landed safely at the airport. After they were on the ground, the co-pilot asked how the sign helped him determine their position.

"I knew it had to be the Microsoft building," the pilot replied, "because like any computer company's help staff, they gave me a technically correct but completely useless answer."

● LINDA A. TOZER

Sitting at the kitchen table, I idly picked up a pack of cards and laid out a hand of solitaire, a game that I hadn't played in quite a while. My ten-year-old son came by and stopped to admire what I had done.

"Wow!" Zackary said. "You know how to play that without a computer!"

● SARAH NEVILLE

I just set my e-mail's auto-response to "I'm looking into this now. I'll let you know." I literally never have to respond to e-mails again.

● @9TO5LIFE

As a professor at Texas A&M, I taught during the day and did research at night. I would usually take a break around nine, however, calling up the strategy game Warcraft on the Internet and playing with an online team.

One night I was paired with a veteran of the game who was a master strategist. With him at the helm, our troops crushed opponent after opponent, and after six games we were undefeated. Suddenly, my fearless leader informed me his mom wanted him to go to bed.

"How old are you?" I typed.

"Twelve," he replied. "How old are you?"

Feeling my face redden, I answered, "Eight."

● TODD SAYRE, PH.D.

> "The attention span of a computer is only as long as its power cord."
>
> AUTHOR UNKNOWN

I was visiting a friend who could not find her cordless phone. After several minutes of searching, her young daughter said, "You know what they should invent? A phone that stays connected to its base so it never gets lost."

● MIRIAM SCOW

A fellow is having computer problems at work, so he calls the IT department. A technician arrives and asks the man for his password.

"My password is MickeyMinnieGoofyPlutoHueyDewey-LouieDonaldBerlin," the fellow replies.

"Why is it so long?" the technician asks.

"Because," the man replies, "I was told it had to be eight characters and a capital."

● PETER ROGERS

Because Google is so popular, it's conceited. Have you tried misspelling something lately? See the tone that it takes? "Um, did you mean . . . ?"

● ARJ BARKER

There's a picture of Jesus that pops up on my computer screen if I leave it idle for ten minutes. It's my screen savior.

While gardening one afternoon, I observed two four-year-old girls pushing dolls' prams. As they passed me, one said to the other, "I wish I had a real baby and not just a doll."

Her friend replied, "Have you tried the Internet?"

● MANDY HOLTEN

"Lord!" said an angel. "They have discovered the human genome code!"

"Darn hackers!" Jesus exclaimed. "Now I'll have to change the password."

● JOÃO PEDRO GOMES

FRIEND #1: Are you visiting us tomorrow? Do you need directions?

FRIEND #2: I'm all set. I have the address, a GPS, and a GPS override.

FRIEND #1: What's a GPS override?

FRIEND #2: My wife.

● BALASUBRAMANIAN VENKATARAMAN

For their first anniversary, a man buys his young wife a cell phone. She is thrilled and listens eagerly as he explains all its features. The next day she is out shopping when the phone rings.

"Hi, honey," her husband says. "How do you like your new phone?"

"Oh, I just love it!" she gushes. "It's so cute and small—and your voice sounds so clear. But there's just one thing I don't understand."

"What's that?"

"How did you know I was at Wal-Mart?"

● ORVILLE HINZ

I'd been finding it frustratingly difficult to reach my satellite company by phone. Finally I got through at about 6:00 one morning.

"Just how many people answer the phone there?" I asked the operator.

"Hundreds," she replied.

I mouthed this information to my family, rolling my eyes.

"Sure," my eight-year-old said. "But they've only got one phone."

● CATHY ROUETTE

WHEREISTHE**SPACEBAR?**

Working on a cruise ship, I was demonstrating to a group of young passengers how the ship manages to stay level at sea. "Do you know what level means?" I asked my six- to eight-year-old charges.

One boy replied immediately. "A level is something you need to pass in a video game to get to a harder screen."

● CHRISTINA L. AMOS

I was in line to receive Communion one Sunday, when the cellphone of the woman ahead of me went off just as the priest was giving her a wafer. The woman stammered an apology as she fumbled with the phone, trying to turn it off. Without skipping a beat, the priest said, "Tell them we don't do takeout."

● JENNIFER WHITCOMB

A colleague at the airport found a cellphone in one of the boarding areas. She switched it on, hoping a caller would identify the owner. It rang and she answered, but there was no response. When it rang a second time, another woman employee answered it and the same thing happened. Moments later, a supervisor came by and picked up the ringing phone. "This is Bob, may I help you?"

"Bob," the bewildered woman caller finally replied. "Where is Bill, and who are those two women he is with?"

● LAURA SPARKS

Since my sixteen-year-old son recently received a prepaid cellphone as a gift, I've asked him to use it to call home if he's out past his curfew. One Saturday while waiting up for him, I dozed off in front of the TV. Later, I woke to realize that there was no sign of him and no call. Irate, I punched in his number. When he answered I demanded, "Where are you, and why haven't you bothered to phone?"

"Dad," he sleepily replied, "I'm upstairs in bed. I've been home for an hour."

● DON JENTLESON

Something very sad about the fact that I haven't read *Moby Dick*, but I have read the *Kindergarten Cop* Wikipedia page.

● AZIZ ANSARI

Problems with my laptop required calling the dreaded company help line. The service rep, based in another country, did not speak English very well. So I tried to explain it as simply as possible:

"I can't get the computer to work."

"Ah, I see," he responded. "You are unable to transport your computer to your place of employment."

● MARIANNE THOMPSON

As we drove through the Appalachian Mountains in the Allegheny National Forest in Pennsylvania, every bend in the road brought a new vista of mountains and valleys. I was snapping photos from the car window, commenting on the view. Oblivious to it all, my teenage son and his friend were engrossed in a video game. I urged them to enjoy the beauty. Their heads swiveled in tandem as they regarded our surroundings. In unison they muttered, "Wow!" then turned back to their game.

● NANCY RUTH

My four-year-old grandson, Cole, was sounding out words to type into his entertainment gaming system.

"Nama," Cole asked me, "how do you spell 'fur'?"

"F-u-r" I said.

"I know how to spell 'Chris,'" he said. "I'm writing 'Christopher.'"

"Oh, let me see," I said, then went over to look at what he had entered.

On the screen was "Chris the Fur"!

● ROSE BRADY

HE SAID/
SHE SAID

> **"** Behind every great man is a woman rolling her eyes. **"**
>
> JIM CARREY

My husband bought an exercise machine to help him shed a few pounds. He set it up in the basement but didn't use it much, so he moved it to the bedroom. It gathered dust there, too, so he put it in the living room.

Weeks later I asked how it was going. "I was right," he said. "I do get more exercise now. Every time I close the drapes, I have to walk around the machine."

● PHYLLIS OLSON

NEVER GO TO BED ANGRY

g. di Chiarro

7TH DAY WITHOUT SLEEP

After Adam stayed out late a few nights, Eve became suspicious.

"You're running around with another woman—admit it!" she demanded.

"What other woman?" Adam shot back. "You're it!"

That night, Adam was fast asleep when he was awakened by Eve poking him in the chest.

"What are you doing?"

"Counting your ribs."

● WILLIAM HALLIDAY

A man says to a friend, "My wife is on a three-week diet."

"Oh, yeah? How much has she lost so far?" asks his pal. He replies, "Two weeks."

● SOURCE: FUNNY IN CANADA SURVEY

Overheard at my garden-club meeting: "I never knew what compost was until I met my husband."

● MARY HALLER

After we had lunch with another couple, the women went shopping, and the men opted to go sailing. Bad decision—a storm blew in while we men were out on the water.

Making matters worse, the tide had gone out, grounding the boat. We had to climb overboard and shove it back into deep water.

As my friend stood there—ankles deep in muck, muscles straining against the weight of the boat, and rain pelting his face—he grinned broadly and with unmistakable sincerity said, "Sure beats shopping!"

● BOB MEYERSON

A woman had a dream. God appeared to her and said, "I'm going to grant you another 40 years, 8 months and 22 days of life." Well, she woke up and she was too excited. And she thought, If that's gonna happen, I'm gonna get a little bit of work done.

So if you could nip it or tuck it, push it or pull it, she had it done. And, man, she was looking too good. So she decided she was going to take herself out for a night on the town. She was downtown walking across the street and a car ran a red light.

Bam! Hit her, killed her dead.

She woke up in heaven and said,

"Now, God, I don't understand this. You said you'd grant me another 40 years, 8 months and 22 days of life, and here I am standing before you. What's up with that?"

God looked at her and said, "I didn't recognize you."

● TERRI ARNETT

I identify with football players because I know what it's like to spend your whole life training for a large, jewel-encrusted ring.

● COMIC SARAH BLODGETT

For a romantic touch, I washed our sheets with lavender-scented detergent. When my husband got into bed, he sniffed. "What's this?" he asked.

"Guess," I said coyly.

"I have no idea," he said. "It smells like the stuff you use to line the hamster's cage."

● KATHLEEN WATERS

I'd noticed that my sixty-year-old father seemed to be losing his hearing, so I mentioned it to my mother.

"Things haven't changed that much," she said. "Only difference is, before, he didn't listen. Now, he can't."

● DEBORAH KELLY

While doing a crossword puzzle, I asked for my husband's help.

"The word is eight letters long and starts with m, and the clue is 'tiresome sameness.'"

"Monogamy," he answered.

● DONNA VAN NOTE

Shortly before our twenty-fifth wedding anniversary, my husband sent twenty-five long-stemmed yellow roses to me at my office. A few days later, I plucked all the petals and dried them. On the night of our anniversary, I spread the petals over the bed and lay on top of them, wearing only a negligee.

As I'd hoped, I got a reaction from my husband.

When he saw me, he shouted, "Are those potato chips?"

● SUE ATER

I asked my wife, "Where do you want to go for our anniversary?"

She said, "Somewhere I have never been!"

I told her, "How?"

● HENNY YOUNGMAN

Did you ever notice: When you put the two words "The" and "IRS" together, they spell "THEIRS"?

The unsaid part of "This is fascinating!" is "to me."

Patient: "Doctor, before I marry Sarah next Saturday, there's something I'd like to get off my chest."
Doctor: "What's that?"
Patient: "A tattoo saying: 'I love Alice.'"

● JONATHAN SHELDRAKE

It may have been the most romantic statement ever uttered in our courthouse. In between hearings, a wedding was performed. As the newlyweds left the courtroom, the bride nestled up to the groom and cooed, "Isn't it nice to be here when we're not being convicted of something?"

● BRENDA YASKAL

A man is drinking with his wife when out of the blue he announces, "I love you."
"Is that you or your beer talking?" she asks.
"It's me," he says, "talking to the beer."

I was a mess. My career as an artist was going nowhere, my horseback riding was no longer fulfilling, and in general I felt unattractive. My husband did his best to be supportive: "You're a great artist," "You're a wonderful equestrian," "You're the most beautiful woman I know."

One day, after another bad ride, I told him my horse seemed depressed. "How do I cheer up a horse?" I asked.

He shared his secret: "Tell her she's good at stuff and that she looks beautiful."

● AMY ACKERMAN

Even though there was a blizzard raging outside, I made it the half-mile to the bakery, where I asked the owner for six rolls.

"Your wife must like rolls," he said.

"How do you know these are for my wife?" I asked.

"Because your mother wouldn't send you out in weather like this."

● RICHARD SILBERLUST

A customer at a coffee shop was clearly peeved by the text message he'd just received. "You ever have that ex-girlfriend who just won't go away?" he asked his friend.

"Yeah," came the reply. "My wife."

● JAMES BAVA

FOR RICHER AND **FOR POORER**

"When I married Donna, I could get both hands around her waist," said my husband's grandfather. Pointing at his full-figured wife, he boasted, "Now look how much I got. That's what I call an investment!"

● KATHERINE EBY

A fourth marriage meant yet another name change for me. I didn't realize the upheaval it had caused until I asked my father why I hadn't heard from him in a while.

"I forgot your phone number," he said.

"You could've looked it up in the phone book."

"I didn't know what name to look under."

● CAROL MARSH

Every night, Harry goes out drinking. And every night, his wife, Louise, yells at him. One day, one of Louise's friends suggests that she try a different tack. "Welcome him home with a kiss and some loving words," she says. "He might change his ways."

That night, Harry stumbles back home as usual. But instead of berating him, Louise helps him into an easy chair, puts his feet up on the ottoman, removes his shoes, and gently massages his neck.

"It's late," she whispers. "I think we should go upstairs to bed now, don't you?"

"Might as well," says Harry. "I'll get in trouble if I go home."

As I picked out flowers for my mother, I noticed a man next to me juggling three boxes of candy and a large bouquet.

"What did you do wrong?" I said with a laugh.

He mumbled back, "I got married."

● BRENDA RHODES

Clearly, my husband and I need to brush up on our flirting. The other night, after I crawled into bed next to him, he wrapped his large arms around me, drew a deep breath, and whispered, "Mmm . . . that Vicks smells good."

● REBECCA RIZZUTI

I turned to my father one night and said, "It's amazing—50 years and you never once had an affair. How do you account for that?"

He replied, "I can't drive."

● CAITLIN FLANAGAN

"WHAT?! . . . I'm multi-tasking!"

An item on Craigslist: "Antique sewing table refinished by my wife, $30. If she's home, $100."

The wheel of my grocery cart was making a horrible scraping sound as I rolled it through the supermarket. Nevertheless, when I finished my shopping and saw a cartless woman, I offered it up, explaining, "It makes an awful noise, but it works."

"That's okay," she said, taking it. "I have a husband at home like that."

● DONNA ULREY

Halfway through a romantic dinner, my husband smiled and said, "You look so beautiful under these lights." I was falling in love all over again when he added, "We gotta get some of these lights."

● SHAWNNA COFFEY

I'm still in my first marriage. I know it's wrong to talk about it so temporary like that. My current husband hates it when I do that.

● OPHIRA EISENBERG

When my petite mother found her seat on the airplane, she was crushed between my 200-plus-pound father and another large man.

"I bet you wish you'd married a smaller man," my father said.

My mother mumbled, "I did."

● JUDITH SEYFERT

If you have a boat and a happy marriage, you don't need another thing.

● ED MCMAHON

At my granddaughter's wedding, the DJ polled the guests to see who had been married the longest. Since it turned out to be my husband and me, the DJ asked us, "What advice would you give to the newly married couple?"

I said, "The three most important words in a marriage are, 'You're probably right.'"

Everyone then looked expectantly at my husband. "She's probably right," he said.

● BARBARA HANCOCK

> The wisest married men give in early. They get in touch with the wife side of themselves, and that's when they stop arguing.
>
> BILL COSBY

There are women whose thoughtful husbands buy them flowers for no reason. And then there's me. One day I couldn't stand it any longer. "Why don't you ever bring me flowers?" I asked.

"What's the point?" my husband said. "They die after about a week."

"So could you," I shot back, "but I still like having you around."

● KAY STRAYER

My cell phone quit as I tried to let my wife know that I was caught in freeway gridlock and would be late for our anniversary dinner. I wrote a message on my laptop asking other motorists to call her, printed it on a portable inkjet and taped it to my rear windshield.

When I finally arrived home, my wife gave me the longest kiss ever. "I really think you love me," she said. "At least 70 people called and told me so."

● JARON SUMMERS

"If this relationship's gonna work, you gotta give me some space."

My husband is wonderful with our baby daughter, but often turns to me for advice. Recently I was in the shower when he poked his head in to ask, "What should I feed Lily for lunch?"

"That's up to you," I replied. "There's all kinds of food. Why don't you pretend I'm not home?"

A few minutes later, my cell phone rang. I answered it to hear my husband saying, "Yeah, hi, honey. Uh . . . what should I feed Lily for lunch?"

● JULLIE BALL

I was leafing through one of my hunting catalogs when I found something that made me laugh. "Look," I said to my wife. "What I've always wanted: a camouflage toilet seat."

"Get it," she said. "Then you'll have an excuse for when you miss."

● MICHAEL KRETZLER

My granddaughter asked why I called my husband Hon.

"It's a term of endearment," I explained.

My husband mumbled, "After more than 40 years, it's a term of endurement."

● MARILY KLATT

A man rushed to the jewelry counter in the store where I work soon after the doors opened one morning and said he needed a pair of diamond earrings. I showed him a wide selection, and quickly he picked out a pair.

When I asked him if he wanted the earrings gift-wrapped, he said, "That'd be great. But can you make it quick? I forgot today was my anniversary, and my wife thinks I'm taking out the trash."

● ANDRE F. PAYSON II

My friend was at the beauty parlor when she overheard another woman rattle on to the manicurist about the sad state of her marriage.

"Things have gotten so bad," she said, "I think I might ask for a divorce. What do you think?"

"That's a serious matter," came the reply. "I think you should consult another manicurist."

● NATALIE ISAACS

My wife and I were having a very hypothetical discussion: In the unlikely event that Hollywood made a movie based on our lives, we wondered what stars would play us.

"Who would you pick to portray you?" she asked me.

I thought about it for a minute, then answered, "Dennis Quaid."

"In that case," she said, "I'll play myself."

● MARK SUGGS

One of my customers at the department of motor vehicles wanted a personalized license plate with his wedding anniversary on it. As we completed the paperwork he explained, "This way I can't forget the date."

A few hours later, I recognized the same young man waiting in my line. When his turn came, he said somewhat sheepishly, "I need to change the numbers on that plate application."

● N. V. GOODMAN

The lawyer I work for specializes in divorce cases, so I was a little surprised to get a call from a prisoner serving life for murdering his wife. My boss was surprised too.

"What does he need me for?" he asked. "He appears to have solved all his marital problems by himself."

● RHONDA CHANG

As the music swelled during a recent wedding reception, my hopelessly romantic husband squeezed my hand, leaned in, and said, "You are better looking than half the women here."

● MARLENE BAMBRICK

IN SICKNESS AND **IN HEALTH**

To our shock and horror, my sister-in-law and I realized we had each been married nearly 50 years. "That's a long time," I observed.

"A long, long time," she agreed. Then she smiled. "Something just occurred to me."

"What's that?"

"If I had killed your brother the first time I felt like it, I'd be out of jail by now."

● BARBARA MASON

One day my housework-challenged husband decided to wash his sweatshirt. Seconds after he stepped into the laundry room, he shouted to me, "What setting do I use on the washing machine?"

It depends," I replied. "What does it say on your shirt?"

"University of Oklahoma," he yelled back.

● JERRI BOYER

"That's a nice plant," said a woman at the florist's shop, pointing to the flower I was buying.

"Yeah, my wife and I had an argument," I admitted. "I was going to buy her a dozen roses, but I don't think she's that mad at me."

● ART FLAGEL

If the marriage needs help, the answer almost always is have more fun. Drop your list of grievances and go ride a roller coaster.

● GARRISON KEILLOR

Pregnant with our second child, I was determined to ride my exercise bike at least two miles a day. Late one night, having put it off all day, I climbed aboard the noisy contraption in our bedroom, where my husband was reading a book.

After about twenty minutes of listening to the squeaky machine, he glanced up, somewhat annoyed. "Don't you think it's time you turned around and headed for home?" he asked.

● MARGARET KOCH

My friend's husband is always telling her that housekeeping would be a snap if only she would organize her time better. Recently he had a chance to put his theory into practice while his wife was away.

When I popped in one evening to see how he was managing, he crowed, "I made a cake, frosted it, washed the kitchen windows, cleaned all the cupboards, scrubbed the kitchen floor, walls and ceiling and even had a bath."

I was about to concede that perhaps he was a better manager than his wife, when he added sheepishly, "When I was making the chocolate frosting, I forgot to turn off the mixer before taking the beaters out of the bowl, so I had to do all the rest."

● MARY L. COSTAIN

All eyes were on him when he said, "Oh, Cindy and I met in college. We were matched up by a computer according to compatibility."

"That's the whole story?" my wife asked incredulously.

"Oh, no," he replied with a grin. "They've fixed the computer since then."

● JOHN MORRISSEY

Although I was only a few pounds overweight, my wife was harping on me to diet. One evening we took a brisk walk downtown, and I surprised her by jumping over a parking meter, leapfrog style.

Pleased with myself, I said, "How many fat men do you know who can do that?"

"One," she retorted.

● R. T. MCLAURY

j. di Chiarro

"You've done something different with your hair."

Torrential rains soaked South Louisiana and flood waters were six feet high. Mrs. Boudreaux was sitting on her roof with her neighbor Mrs. Thibodaux, waiting for help to come. Mrs. Thibodaux spied a lone baseball cap floating near the house. The cap seemed to be moving back and forth slowly but steadily. "Do you see that baseball cap?" she asked Mrs. Boudreaux.

"Oh, yes, that's my husband," Mrs. Boudreaux replied. "I told him he was going to cut the grass today come hell or high water."

● MONIQUE HENDERSON

My mother and I were having a mother-daughter talk about the qualities to look for in a husband. She stressed that husband and wife should be as much alike as possible in interests and backgrounds. I brought up the point that opposites often attract.

"Diane," she said emphatically, "just being man and woman is opposite enough."

● DIANE RENZI

A man and his wife were taking an afternoon drive through the countryside. They had just had a big argument and were not talking to one another. Finally the husband decided to break the silence and say something sarcastic to his wife: "Look at all the cows and pigs in the pasture. Don't they remind you of your relatives?"

The wife replied, "Yes, they do. They remind me of my in-laws."

A wife asks her husband, "Could you please go shopping for me and buy one carton of milk and, if they have avocados, get six."

A short time later, the husband returns with six cartons of milk. "Why did you buy six cartons of milk?" his wife asks.

He replies, "They had avocados."

● TOM BUOYE

I was in my ninth month of pregnancy and feeling very uncomfortable. On top of everything, my pleas for sympathy seemed to go unnoticed by my husband.

One day I told him, "I hope in your next life you get to be pregnant!"

He replied, "I hope in your next life you get to be married to someone who's pregnant!"

● PATTI COOK

During an attack of laryngitis I lost my voice completely for two days. To help me communicate with him, my husband devised a system of taps.

One tap meant "Give me a kiss." Two taps meant "No." Three taps meant "Yes"—and 95 taps meant "Take out the garbage."

● MILDRED BALDWIN

You know you're dating the wrong guy when your friend steals your boyfriend and all you can think is, What does she see in him?

My wife and I were comparing notes the other day. "I have a higher IQ, did better on my SATs and make more money than you," she pointed out.

"Yeah, but when you step back and look at the big picture, I'm still ahead," I said.

She looked mystified. "How do you figure?"

"I married better," I replied.

● LOUIS RODOLICO

Soon after we were married, my husband, Paul, stopped wearing his wedding band.

"Why don't you ever wear your ring?" I asked.

"It cuts off my circulation," Paul replied.

"I know," I said. "It's supposed to."

● MARILY WARE

As I was stepping into the shower after an afternoon of yard work, my wife walked into the bathroom. "What do you think the neighbors would say if I cut the grass dressed like this?" I asked.

Giving me a casual glance, she replied, "They'd say I married you for your money."

● JOHN R. BUCO

Like all parents, my husband and I just do the best we can, and hold our breath and hope we've set aside enough money for our kids' therapy.

● MICHELLE PFEIFFER

A man tells his doctor that he's incapable of doing all the things around the house that he used to do. When the examination is over, he says, "Okay, Doctor. In plain English—what's wrong with me?"

"Well, in plain English," says the doctor, "you're just lazy."

The man nods. "Now give me the medical term so I can tell my wife."

● EDSEL BASCO

> I take my wife everywhere, but she keeps finding her way back.
>
> HENNY YOUNGMAN

When a woman in my office became engaged, a colleague offered her some advice. "The first ten years are the hardest," she said.

"How long have you been married?" I asked.

"Ten years," she replied.

● TONYA WINTER

As I stripped off my sweatshirt at the breakfast table one warm morning, my T-shirt started to come off too.

My husband let out a low whistle. I took it as a compliment until he said, from behind his newspaper, "Can you believe the price of bananas?"

● BEATRICE ROCHE

What to engrave on the inside of my husband-to-be's wedding ring?

I turned to my sister and said, "I want something that has meaning and will remind him of me."

Her suggestion?

"Put it back on."

● TRACI WILLIAMS

One evening my daughter, Shayna, wondered: "What would happen if Daddy died? Would you get married again?"

"I don't think so, honey," I replied. "It's hard to imagine loving anyone as much as I love Daddy."

"What about Daddy?" my son Isaac asked. "Would he get married again?"

"Well, of course!" Shayna blurted. "He'd need someone to do the laundry."

● MICHELLE HOLMES

A DAY IN THE LIFE

" If the customer is always right, why isn't everything free? **"**

"I'm an intern."

SERVICE WITH **A SMILE**

A few weeks back, I went to the hardware store and bought an ax to use on an overgrown shrub. I put the ax in a bag and went a few doors down to the grocery store, where I bought two bottles of wine. As the clerk placed the wine in the bag, he spotted the ax. "This," he said, "has all the makings of a very interesting weekend."

● LYLE BREWER

"What are you doing?" asked my mother after I pressed several buttons on her microwave.

"Reheating these leftovers for two minutes at 80 percent."

"I didn't know you could do that."

"Sure. How do you reheat bacon?"

"Oh," she said, "that's two biscuits and a popcorn."

● ROBIN ROBERSON

A man is woken up by a knock at the door one morning. He gets up and goes downstairs to open the door and is met by a six-foot-six-inch spider who immediately head-butts him, runs inside, tramples all over the man, kicks him in the back, boots his ribs and stamps all over him.

Next thing the homeowner remembers is waking up in hospital. Turning to the doctor he says, "I feel terrible. What's wrong with me?"

"Don't worry, everything's all right," the doctor tells him. "It's just a vicious bug going about."

● PHIL MURPHY

I worked as a maid for an elderly lady who sometimes got things mixed up. A couple of days before Christmas, just before she left for an appointment, she asked me to take down her Halloween decorations and then lock up. I assumed she had mixed up the holidays, and although I thought it rather odd, I took the Christmas decorations down. Later that day she phoned me at home.

"What have you done?" she asked.

"Took down the decorations," I replied, "just as you asked."

Laughing, she said, "The cobwebs, dear."

● MICHELLE ROGERS

Our normally sweet Great Dane has one quirk: She hates United Parcel Service drivers. While walking her one day, we came upon a guy delivering a package. Struggling to keep hold of her, I joked, "As you can see, she just loves UPS men."

Circumnavigating us, he muttered, "Don't you feed her anything else?"

● DONALD DAWSON

A man is visiting an old friend when a little girl races through the room. "Diploma," the friend calls after her, "bring us two cups of coffee."

"Diploma? What an odd name," says the visitor. "How did she get it?"

The friend sighs. "I sent my daughter to study at the university in Lisbon, and that's what she came back with."

● SOURCE: FUNNY IN PORTUGAL SURVEY

My wife is a very adventurous cook. "How does this sound?" she called out from the kitchen. "Bonito, surimi, and anchovies in a decadent, silky broth."

"Sounds delicious," I hollered back. "Is that what we're having tonight?"

"No. I'm reading from this packet of cat food."

● DAVID WELLINGS

A customer walked up to my bank window and asked me to cash a check.

"Of course," I said. "But I'll need to see ID."

She dug though her purse and handed me a snapshot. "That's me in the middle," she said.

● DEBORAH BERKLEY

One of my insurance customers faxed over the police report from an auto accident. Several weeks later, she called asking for information from that report. "Didn't you keep the original copy?" I asked.

"No," she said. "I faxed it to you."

● SHERRI SMITH

My sister got a call from a telemarketer who was selling replacement windows. "I can't use them," she said. "I'm renting an apartment."

"No problem," he said. "You can take the windows with you when you move."

● LAURA O'NEAL

When someone tells you that something defies description, you can be pretty sure he's going to have a go at it anyway.

My husband and I arrived at the auto dealership to pick up our new car, only to be told that the keys had been locked inside. We went to the service department, where a mechanic was working to unlock the driver's side door. Instinctively, I reached for the passenger door and—voilà!—it was unlocked. "Hey," I shouted to him. "It's open!"

"I know," yelled the mechanic. "I already got that side. Now I'm working on this door."

● BETTY M. PHILLIPS

When I stepped on the scale at my doctor's office, I was surprised to see that I weighed 144 pounds. "Why don't you just take off that last four?" I joked to the nurse's aide as she made a notation on my chart. A few moments later, my doctor came in and flipped through the chart.

"I see you've lost weight," he said. "You're down to 14 pounds."

● RACHEL WAGNER

JUST GETTING
THROUGH THE DAY

Having avoided the scale for a few years, my husband finally got up the nerve to climb aboard. Unable to read the numbers, he got off to grab his eyeglasses and stepped back on.

"What do you know?" he called out. "These glasses weigh fifty pounds."

● ERMA TIMPSON

**"Remember 'No Child Left Behind'?
Well, obviously, the bus driver doesn't."**

Occasionally at the restaurant where I work there are extra desserts, and the staff are given some to take home. Once I brought home two pieces of cheesecake for my son and daughter. Katie had a piece that evening.

The next day her older brother found her watching TV and eating more cheesecake. "Are you eating my cheesecake?" he demanded.

"Oh, no," she replied sweetly, "I ate yours yesterday."

● BRENDA GINGRICH

My friend read her son's horoscope and thought it quite appropriate. "You've spent the last few weeks looking for escape," it said. "But now it's time to get on with your life."

She had just given birth to him that morning.

● SUYEE KAOR

Recently as I approached a stop sign, I hit a patch of ice and lightly bumped the car in front of me. There was no damage, but the other driver and I decided to exchange information anyway. I got back into my car to look for paper, and my seven-year-old son, Matthew, asked what I was doing. "I'm just exchanging names and phone numbers with the other driver," I explained.

When I returned to the car, Matthew asked, "So, what's our new name and phone number?"

● SHERRI ADAMSON

My husband met me at the doctor's office for my routine checkup, and from there we decided to go out to eat. Since we had driven in separate cars, I arrived at the restaurant first.

"One for dinner?" asked the hostess.

"No," I replied. "There will be two of us in just a minute."

When I saw the panicky look on the hostess's face, I realized I had forgotten about my appearance. Anybody could see that I was at least 8 1/2 months pregnant.

● LOANN K. BURKE

I ate a gluten-free, lactose-free, low-carb pizza
for dinner tonight. (It was a raw tomato.)
● @SAMIR

While phoning a friend, my grandmother dialed the wrong number. She apologized and tried again, but she got the same number. Once more she hung up and redialed—same result. Now Grandma was frustrated.

"Look," she told the person on the other end, "I'm going to call my friend again. This time, don't answer her phone!"

● DANIELLE GILLELAND

> Some sad news from Australia . . . the inventor of the boomerang grenade died today.
>
> JOHNNY CARSON

"Madam, there's no such thing as a tough child—if you parboil them first for seven hours, they always come out tender."

● W.C. FIELDS

A woman walked into my father's carpet store. She'd just moved out of her parents' home and needed something for her new living-room floor. "Do you know how big the room is?" Dad asked.

"Yes," she said. "It's 22 flip-flops long by 18 flip-flops wide. And I wear a size 8."

● REGENIA SADBERRY

My husband was driving home from work when he was pulled over for not wearing a seat belt. Two days later—same ticket, same cop.

"So," the officer said, "have you learned anything?"

"Yes, I have," said my husband. "I've learned I need to take a different way home from work."

● KIMBERLY OWEN

"No, this video of your father jogging is
not in slow motion."

When my daughter asked her husband to take over watching their three-year-old son during his bath, Wyatt, my grandson, instead told her to stay. Laughing, she asked how many adults it took to keep an eye on him.

He answered, "One to watch me and one to pick up the broken stuff!"

● CHARMAINE HUCULAK

One day we were watching a game, when my mother-in-law shrieked from the kitchen, "Jim, there's a horsefly in here!"

Not taking his eyes off the screen, he barked back, "Give it some cough syrup."

● JEFF STEWART

JUST FOR **LAUGHS**

After our parents retired, they moved from a busy city in Rhode Island to a small town in Maine. We didn't realize how small the town was until my sister visited the local video store. She selected a movie and told the clerk that she was going to rent the cassette under her parents' name.

The clerk looked at the title and replied, "They already saw that one."

● THERESA COUTCHER SOKOLOWSKI

One night, telephone solicitors kept interrupting our supper. When the phone rang yet again, my father answered it. By his remarks, we assumed it was his friend Ed, a notorious practical joker.

Dad kept saying things like, "Cut it out, Ed. This is very funny, but I know it's you. C'mon, stop it or I'll hang up. I'll get you for this."

When Dad hung up, my mom asked, "Was that Ed?"

"No," my father replied. "It was a salesman, and I don't think he'll call back."

● TONI M. VIDRA

I was lying on my couch, burning up with a fever, when my husband said I should go to bed. At 3 A.M. the next morning, I woke up soaked from head to toe. When my husband heard me stirring, he said that my fever must have broken.

I decided to spend the rest of the night back on the couch so as not to disturb him any further. But then, three hours later, he appeared in the living room soaking wet. "Your fever didn't break," he said, still dripping. "The water bed did."

● SUSAN BARR

At age seventy, my grandfather bought his first riding lawn mower.

"This thing is great," he bragged to my brother. "It took me only an hour and a half to mow the lawn. It used to take your grandmother two days to do it all!"

● DIANE HARDY

During a home renovation, my grandfather was watching me drive in nails. "You hammer like lightning," he said.

"Really?" I replied, flattered.

"You never strike the same place twice."

● DAVE LOCKETT

When my wife called a friend on our touch-tone phone, the line was busy. She tried several more times, but without success. Watching her, I asked why she wasn't using the redial button.

"Honey," she answered, "I need the exercise."

● HENRY H. POLITZER

My mom moved into a new condo, and I went to visit for a couple of days. Searching for a coffee cup one morning, I sighed, "It seems like I'm always looking for something in your kitchen."

"That's good," Mom said. When I looked confused, she explained, "Because when you know where to look, it's time to go home."

● CAROLINE YOUNG

Our day-care center spent time helping the kids memorize their home addresses. My daughter, who was in my class, had her street name down, but couldn't remember the house number.

"If our house is on fire and you call 911," I asked, "how will the firefighters know where to go?"

She had a plan: "I'll tell them to go to South 14th Street and look for the house that's on fire."

● DIANNA PHYFER

NEW DEFINITIONS TO ADD TO YOUR VOCABULARY:

- **Arbitrator:** A cook that leaves Arby's to work at McDonald's.
- **Bernadette:** The act of torching your mortgage.
- **Parasites:** What you see from the top of the Eiffel Tower.
- **Primate:** Removing your spouse from in front of the TV.
- **Subdued:** A guy that works on submarines.

● EDWARD THOMPSON

Did you hear about the dyslexic, agnostic, insomniac? He stayed up all night trying to decide if there really was a dog!

Although I knew I had put on a few pounds, I didn't consider myself overweight until the day I decided to clean my refrigerator. I sat on a chair in front of the appliance and reached in to wipe the back wall.

While I was in this position, my teenage son came into the kitchen. "Hi, Mom," he said. "Whatcha doin', having lunch?"

I started my diet that day.

● BETTY STROHM

Our son lived at home all four of his undergraduate years. He moved out only when he went to grad school and got an apartment. The first time my husband and I went to see his new place, Matt greeted us, saying, "I'm glad to finally be the host."

As we walked in the door, my husband whispered to me, "Instead of the parasite."

● DIANNE GARDNER

My young son declared, "When I grow up, I'm going to marry you, Mommy."

"You can't marry your own mother," said his older sister.

"Then I'll marry you."

"You can't marry me either."

He looked confused, so I explained, "You can't marry someone in your own family."

"You mean I have to marry a total stranger?!" he cried.

● PHLYLIS SHOWERS

Don't sweat the petty things, and don't pet the sweaty things.

"We never should have called it the pup tent."

When my four-year-old son got on his first bicycle, I told him, "Step back on the pedals and the bike will brake."

He nodded, then proceeded to ride straight into a bush.

"Why didn't you push back on the pedals?" I asked, helping him up.

"You said that if I did, the bike would break."

When I announced that I was getting married, my excited mother said, "You have to have the rehearsal dinner someplace opulent, where there's dancing."

My father, seeing where this was heading, said, "I'll pay you a thousand dollars to elope."

"And you have to have a breakfast, for the people who are coming from out of town."

"Two thousand."

"We'll need a photographer. Oh, and what colors do you want for the reception?"

"Five thousand!"

We eloped to Spain.

● MARY NICHOLS

I asked my brother-in-law, the father of four boys, "If you had it to do all over again, would you still have kids?"

"Yes," he said. "Just not these four."

● SHEILA LEE,

Before you marry a person, you should first make them use a computer with slow Internet to see who they really are.

● WILL FERRELL

After sailing across the Atlantic, my family and I arrived in France. Wanting directions and sorely in need of conversation, my father stopped a passerby and asked if he spoke English. Sizing up my disheveled father, the man warily responded, "Sometimes."

● KATHERINE TUCKER

ONE FOR THE **ROAD**

Three guys are talking about what constitutes fame. The first guy defines it as being invited to the White House for a chat with the president.

"Nah," says the second guy. "Real fame would be if the red phone rang when you were there, and the president wouldn't take the call."

"You're both wrong," says the third. "Fame is when you're in the Oval Office and the red phone rings, the president answers it, listens for a second, and then says, "It's for you."

● PATTIE BROWNE

Service in the restaurant was abysmally slow. My husband was starting to flip out, so I tried to distract him with small talk.

"You know," I said, "our friend Christi should be having her baby anytime now."

"Really?" my husband snapped. "She wasn't even pregnant when we walked in here."

● MAUREEN MORRISON

Three and a half agonizing hours at the Department of Motor Vehicles put me in a foul mood. I was still in a funk when I stopped at a store to buy a baseball bat for my son. "Cash or charge?" the young woman clerk asked.

"Cash," I snapped. Then I quickly apologized. "I'm sorry. I just spent half the day in line at the DMV."

"Would you like me to wrap the bat," she chirped, "or do you plan to go back?"

● ADRIEN D.

"It's my new RING TONE!"

"You gotta do something," Farmer John told the sheriff. "Speeders are killing my chickens."

The next day, workers erected a sign near the farm: Slow—School Crossing.

Three days later, John called again. "That sign's not helping. Folks ignore it."

So the sheriff sent out workers with a new sign: Slow—Children at Play.

Three days later, Farmer John picked up the phone again. "Can I make my own sign?"

The sheriff agreed. Three weeks later, he called to check on John. "How's the new sign working out for you?" he asked.

"Great!" the farmer replied. "Not one chicken has been killed since I put it up."

Thinking such an effective sign might be useful elsewhere, the sheriff went to see it. The new sign read: Nudist Colony—Go slow and watch for chicks.

One weekend, car horns sounded after a wedding near our home. Charlie, my five-year-old, asked me what was happening. "People like to beep their horns after a couple is married," I explained.

"Why?" he wondered. "Is it a warning?"

● DIANE WILSON

A friend and I were hitchhiking, but no one would stop. "Maybe it's our long hair," I joked. With that, my friend scrawled on a piece of cardboard: "Going to the barber's." Within seconds we had our ride.

● RAYMOND BUTKUS

The minute I walked into the post office, the postmaster noticed the new earrings my husband had given me.

"Those must be real diamonds," she said.

"Yes," I said. "How could you tell?"

"Because," she said, "no one buys fake diamonds that small."

● DEBORAH CAUDELL

When I enlisted in my teens, I took up smoking cigars to make myself look more mature. Did it work? Well, one time, as I proudly puffed away at our NCO club, an older sergeant growled, "Hey, kid, your candy bar's on fire."

● JAMES BUSHART

I was waiting with my brother, Sid, at the doctor's office. When the receptionist pulled Sid's file, she noted there were two files with the same name. He explained that he and his father had the same name, but that his father had passed away.

The receptionist said, "So one of you is dead and the other isn't."

"That is correct," Sid said.

"Which one are you?" she asked, pointing to the files.

"The live one, I hope!" Sid replied.

● DEBORAH STERN

If you stop eating doughnuts you will live three years longer, but it's just three more years that you'll want a doughnut.

● LEWIS BLACK

While at a convention, Bill, Jim, and Scott shared a hotel suite on the 75th floor. After a long day of meetings, they were shocked to find that the hotel elevators were broken and that they'd have to climb all the way up to their room.

"I have a way to break the monotony," said Bill. "I'll tell jokes for 25 flights, Jim can sing songs for the next 25, and Scott can tell sad stories the rest of the way."

As they started walking up, Bill told his first joke. At the 26th floor, Jim began to sing. At the 51st floor, it was Scott's turn.

"I will tell my saddest story first," he said. "Once there was a man who left the room key in the car."

● NOAH JORGENSEN

> As soon as the hospital made me put on one of those little gowns, I knew the end was in sight.
>
> ADAM JOSHUA SMARGON

During a lesson, my driving instructor commented that he was seeing spots before his eyes.

Deeply concerned, I told him how my father had suffered a detached retina a few years earlier and had complained of similar symptoms prior to diagnosis.

"This could be very serious," I said. "You must see a doctor immediately."

"Or you could just turn the windshield wipers on," replied the instructor.

● MARTIN ROSE

SCENE: A MAN APPLYING FOR CREDIT AT A DEPARTMENT STORE.

Clerk: What do you do for a living?
Man: I'm a tree trimmer.
Clerk: What do you do after Christmas?

● RUTH SADECKAS

Also Available from Reader's Digest

Laughter, the Best Medicine

Drawn from one of the most popular features of *Reader's Digest* magazine, this lighthearted collection of jokes, one-liners, and other glimpses of life is just what the doctor ordered.

ISBN 978-0-89577-977-9 • $9.95 paperback

Laughter Really Is the Best Medicine

Guaranteed to put laughter in your day, this side-splitting compilation of jokes pokes fun at the facts and foibles of daily routines. This little volume is sure to tickle your funny bone.

ISBN 978-1-60652-204-2 • $9.95 paperback

Laughter Still Is the Best Medicine

This hilarious collection offers up some of the funniest moments that get us through our day, with jokes, gags, and cartoons that will have readers laughing out loud.

ISBN 978-1-62145-137-2 • $9.99 paperback

Laughter Totally is the Best Medicine

More than 1,000 of the funniest, laugh-out-loud jokes, quips, quotes, anecdotes, and cartoons from Reader's digest magazine—guaranteed to put laughter in your day.

ISBN 978-1-62145-406-9 • $9.99 paperback

For more information, visit us at RDTradePublishing.com
E-book editions are also available.

Reader's Digest books can be purchased through retail and online bookstores.